Social Psychology
of the
Work Organization

Arnold S. Tannenbaum
The University of Michigan

Wadsworth Publishing Company, Inc.
Belmont, California

Tavistock Publications, Ltd.
London

L.C. Cat. Card No.: 66–16965
Printed in the United States of America

Published simultaneously in Great Britain by Tavistock Publications, Ltd., London

Fourth printing: July 1968

foreword

The heterogeneity of behavioral science in industry makes it impossible for a single author to do justice to the subject's many facets in a single text. Although full-length volumes on particular topics are available for the specialist, these books are often beyond the level of the advanced undergraduate or beginning graduate student, and they typically go into more detail than is justified in a general course. To meet the changing educational needs generated by this complex subject matter, the Behavioral Science in Industry series was conceived.

The concept is simple. Leading authorities have written short books, at a fairly basic level, to present the essentials of particular fields of inquiry. These books are designed to be used in combination, as a basic text for courses in industrial psychology or behavioral science in industry, or singly, as supplementary texts or collateral reading in more specialized courses.

To implement this concept, the editor outlined the general scope of the series, specified a list of titles, and sketched the content of each volume. Leading social scientists nominated authors for each of the proposed books, and, in following up these leads, the editor was extremely fortunate in enlisting the enthusiastic cooperation of the kinds of men who are not only specialists in their subjects, but who can communicate their ideas in highly readable fashion.

The need for such a series is apparent from the marked changes that have occurred in the last two or three decades in the application of the scientific method to the study of human behavior at work. Perhaps the most significant of these changes is the extension of the range of problems subjected to systematic research. The continuing concern of industrial psychology with methods of assessing individual differences for the selection and placement of personnel has been supplemented by intensive research on such diverse topics as leadership and supervision, the design of man-machine systems, consumer preferences, management development, career patterns, and union-management relations.

This expanding focus of industrial psychology has been accompanied by changes in the objectives and strategies of research. Research has become less concerned with techniques for solving particular problems and more concerned with shedding light on the processes that underlie various behavioral phenomena, on the assumption that improvements in technology will be facilitated by a better understanding of these processes. To implement these new objectives, the psychometric and correlational methods of research in personnel selection and placement were adapted to new problems and supplemented by experiments in laboratory and field settings. As a result, the study of behavior in industrial organizations has been undertaken by researchers who have not previously been identified with industrial psychology. Experimental psychologists investigated problems of human factors in equipment design; social psychologists worked on problems of leadership, communication, and social influence; and clinical psychologists applied their diagnostic and therapeutic skills in industrial settings.

The net effect has been a blurring of the boundary lines among these subdisciplines and a growing recognition of the interdependence of "basic" and "applied" research. These changes have also obscured lines of demarcation among disciplines and professions. Psychologists, sociologists, cultural anthropologists, political scientists, and economists, and specialists in such functional managerial fields as production, labor relations, marketing, and accounting have discovered that much of their work is interrelated and that their interests are often mutual. The resultant cross-fertilization has given an interdisciplinary character to much of the new research and has afforded some currency to the interdisciplinary label *behavioral science*.

This series has been planned to reflect these changes in subject matter and research methods and to provide the reader with a valuable summary of the current status of behavioral science in industry.

Victor H. Vroom

preface

This book is intended as an introduction to the social psychology of work organizations—organizations like automobile companies, textile factories, steel mills, electric power plants, and armies. Our topic of interest is the relationship of man to the organization in which he works; his sense of satisfaction, involvement, feelings of identification or loyalty, conflicts, and tensions—as well as his effort in support of, or in opposition to, the formally defined goals of the organization. To a significant extent, the social and psychological research to which we shall refer is concerned with the factors that affect the above reactions and adjustments of members. This research has been done mainly in organizations; however, we want also to consider some research from other settings, including the psychological laboratory.

In the first chapter we try to answer the question "What is organization?" by describing the way that organizations are expected to function. Organizations, in fact, do not work precisely the way they should, but the idealization we present is a useful starting point. It parallels in a number of respects some classical models drawn from the literature of sociology and public administration, which we also discuss. These models portray organization as a highly rational and impersonal system in which the psychology of members is almost completely ignored. Members are taken for granted; they are expected to "fit" and not get in the way of the grand design of the organization.

In Chapter 2 we turn to one serious attempt to take the human factor into account through an approach called *scientific management*. However, this approach oversimplifies human nature by assuming that people are motivated primarily, if not exclusively, by money incentives. Some of the weaknesses of this approach and of the classical sociological and administrative models were revealed through a famous series of experiments started in the 1920s at the Hawthorne plant of the Western Electric Company. These experiments, which we also discuss in Chapter 2, mark one of the beginnings of the human-relations approach to organizations and to a more systematic investigation of psychological factors. We therefore turn in Chapter 3 to a brief discussion of some general but pertinent principles of psychology. A consideration in this chapter of aspects of personality and motivation makes apparent some of the problems of adjustment for many persons in the work organization. These problems are discussed in more detail in subsequent chapters.

Chapters 4 through 7 take up each of four general factors suggested by the Hawthorne study as important in explaining members' performances. Each is considered in the light of the large body of research completed since Hawthorne. Chapter 4 deals with the attitudes, morale, and sense of satisfaction that members derive from their work. It is concerned with some of the conflicts and adjustments which members experience and the possible effect of these conflicts on performance in the organization. In Chapter 5 we see how some of the reactions of members to the organization occur through informal groups and how the behavior of persons is affected by membership in these groups. We review in Chapter 6 a number of studies on supervision and its possible effects on subordinates' motivations and reactions. In Chapter 7 we take up the question of participation—the extent to which members have some control or influence over the conditions that affect them on the job. These chapters illustrate the increasingly interdisciplinary character of the psychologist's approach to organizations. The social psychology of organizations draws upon the work of a number of social sciences: sociology and political and administrative science, as well as psychology.

We are concerned finally, in Chapter 8, with some applications of the knowledge gained through the research described in the previous chapters. How can this knowledge be used to improve organizational performance? This is a most difficult and complex problem. It deals with what we might call organizational engineering or organizational architecture: how to change organizations or how to design them in the first place so that they achieve our purposes most effectively. This task is all the more difficult because it presupposes that men agree about what they want their organizations to do. Unfortunately, they do not always agree, and organizational research is enmeshed in controversy because of the moral and political questions inevitably raised: Will the science of organizations be used for good or ill? Will it be used to manipulate people in subtle and powerful ways, or will it help us to create organizations which are effective and at the same time enriching and fulfilling to members? Our emphasis on science does not mean that we should ignore these moral questions; for organizations, after all, are all about people.

Acknowledgments

The ideas presented in this text are by no means my exclusive property. I have borrowed widely and freely from the writings of many others, as the reader will see. Numbered references in the text represent my acknowledgment and thanks to those whose writings entered directly into my own. My thinking has been influenced, however, in more general ways by several colleagues who, during an association of years, have generously shared with me their ideas about life and research in organizations. To Robert Kahn, Rensis Likert, and Stanley Seashore I therefore express my deep appreciation.

I have also been closely associated during the past several years with a group of colleagues engaged in a program of research and writing on organizations. This research has been supported by a grant from the Carnegie Corporation of New York to the Survey Research Center, Institute for Social Research. This book is one of several products of that program. The members of our research team—Jerald Bachman, Glenn Jones, Dora and Philip Marcus, and Clagett Smith—contributed through many discussions to my understanding of a number of the problems discussed in this text; and Lloyd Morrisett of the Carnegie Corporation provided the kind of understanding support which encouraged us in our joint endeavors. To all of these persons I offer my sincere thanks.

A number of friends and associates in this country and abroad have done me the kindness of reading a draft of this book and of helping me improve that draft: David Bowers, Fred Emery, Glenn Jones, Philip Marcus, Pavle Novosel, Marvin Olsen, Dirk Prins, Stanley Seashore, and Josip Zupanov. Victor Vroom, technical editor of the Wadsworth Behavioral Sciences in Industry Series, also made many helpful suggestions—as did my production editor, Gordon Gilliam.

I am deeply grateful as well to Mary Hope, Joyce Stevens, and Jules van der Maat, who went through with me the tribulations of preparing manuscript for this book. My indebtedness also extends to the Tavistock Institute of Human Relations in London, where I was in residence while part of this text was being written.

contents

The
Work Organization

Industrial and business concerns are complex social organizations designed to produce goods or provide services through the concerted efforts of their members. However, no two organizations are exactly alike. They differ in size, in the goods they produce, and in the technology they employ, and they differ in the social, psychological, and administrative assumptions upon which they are based. These assumptions may be more or less realistic, and the organizations built on them may be more or less successful in achieving the purposes for which they were set up.

Formal and Informal Organization

It is only in relatively recent years that students of organization have analyzed in detail the weaknesses of some of the social and psychological assumptions underlying organizations. A vital distinction has grown out of this analysis, that between *formal* and *informal* organization. The formal organization is the organization that is planned and intended by its designers. Prescribed by rules, it is a kind of official blueprint that reflects the social, psychological, and administrative assumptions of the designers. However, it is never fully realized in the behavior of its members.

The term *informal organization* refers to the unplanned, informal set of groups, friendships, and attachments that inevitably develop when people are placed in regular proximity to one another. These relationships, which grow out of the personal needs of members, are not fully accounted for by the formal organization; in fact, they are sometimes de-signed to protect the members from the demands of the formal organization. The behaviors and sentiments that constitute this informal aspect of organization have no place in the formal plan. Officially, they do not exist. Yet these relationships have a significant effect on the total organizational effort—sometimes to the great chagrin of administrators.

In the next chapter, we shall discuss the importance of the informal organization. Here, we shall consider a number of characteristics that are helpful in describing what the formal work organization is like. Most of these characteristics are essential to the work organization as we know it. All of them are general, in the sense that they are present in some degree in all work organizations. This is the way work organizations *are;* you may want to consider, as you read on, whether this is the way they *have to be.*

Major Characteristics of the Formal Organization

Purpose

The purpose of the work organization is to produce goods or to provide services *efficiently.* We stress the word *efficiently,* because ef-ficiency is instrumental in most work organizations if these organizations are to make profit and hence to survive. The organization may have additional purposes imputed to it by members or by the public; and this has been a subject of some controversy (42, 62, 145). But the need for efficient production is a compelling circumstance, within which most work organizations must function. Even organizations that are sub-sidized or owned by government are expected to perform services or manufacture goods efficiently, and within a budget. The same principle applies widely in communist states, where profit in one form or another, or efficiency, is the measure of organizational success.

Specialization

Organization members necessarily perform different functions; if they all did the same thing, the work of the organization would never get done. In an automobile plant, for example, some members make fenders, others attach these fenders to car bodies, and still others paint the fenders. Hundreds, if not thousands, of workers contribute in their own way to the final product, which may be the Ford or Chrysler or Chevrolet sedan that rolls off the assembly line. This division of labor is not restricted to the production line. There is specialization in the office too; the secretary, the mail boy, the accountant, the engineer, and the lawyer each contributes in special ways to the total work of the organization. At the very pinnacle of the organization, we see specialization reflected in the titles of top executives—for example, vice-presidents in charge of each of several specialties, such as production, sales, industrial relations, planning, research, personnel, and so forth.

Specialization is one of the keys to productive efficiency in modern industrial organization; it is also the source of considerable frustration for many workers. Specialization often requires that jobs be broken into relatively simple components which are performed repetitively. Many industrial jobs are therefore boring; they limit the freedom and initiative of workers and reduce their sense of satisfaction in the work.

Coordination

Specialization creates another problem, one that is its inevitable counterpart in organization: the problem of *coordination*. The many different functions that members perform must be *coordinated* or tied together somehow so that they contribute jointly to the end result. In order for this to be achieved, members have to do the right thing at the right place at the right time; they have to perform their specified tasks so that each contribution fits the contributions of others. Essentially, this means *teamwork*. However, industrial teamwork is a somewhat more complex and subtle kind than that of a basketball team, since many members in a complex organization never see, let alone know, the others with whom they are working.

Order

The ensemble of behaviors in an organization is part of a logical plan to achieve certain formally defined objectives. The success of this plan requires *order*—first, in what goes on within the organization at a particular moment, and, second, in the regularity of the organization through time. Organizations, unlike crowds or other social groupings, which are spontaneous or ephemeral, have *stability and continuity*.

An essential feature of this order is that, within limits, behaviors of and the relations between members are *predictable*. Predictability is the essence of organization, of *organized* action. The behaviors of members are planned, at least in general ways, and unless members conform predictably to expectations, the organization will lapse into anarchy and chaos—which is another way of saying *dis*organization. Suppose a worker who is expected to be on his job from seven to five prefers to be there from eight to six. Such variations are intolerable, especially if they become extensive or chronic.

Authority

Organizations guard against chaos and preserve predictability, orderliness, and regularity through several devices. One such device is the *system of authority.*

Authority is the formal right of a person, by virtue of his position or rank in an organization, to decide, determine, or influence what others in the organization will do. This authority is implemented through a *hierarchy,* or *chain of command,* in which persons at succeedingly higher levels have greater responsibility for ensuring that the members below do what they are supposed to do. In the typical industrial organization, rank-and-file workers are at the bottom of the authority pyramid. They are directed by supervisors, sometimes called *foremen* or *first-line supervisors,* who report to and take directions from still other superiors and so on up the organizational hierarchy.

Uniformity

An important and general implication of the hierarchical system of control is conformity or uniformity in the behaviors of organizational members.

F. H. Allport provided a graphic illustration, through the hypothetical curves shown in Figure 1–1, of the uniformity of behavior implied by organization. The solid-line curve describes the relatively narrow range of behaviors consistent with the requirements of organization. If we consider, for example, the time at which employees arrive at work, we find that the great majority of employees come almost exactly on time; the distribution of arrival times is therefore quite narrow. This uniformity in the behaviors of members contrasts with what one might expect if members were to follow their own purely individualistic inclinations—without regard for organizational requirements. Individuals in this case would arrive at more widely differing times, and their arrivals would probably be distributed as a bell-shaped curve (dashed line), following the usual distribution of personality traits (3).

The narrow, more uniform distribution demonstrates the effects

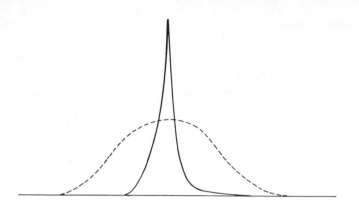

_____ ORGANIZED BEHAVIOR

_ _ _ _ _ INDIVIDUALISTIC BEHAVIOR

FIGURE 1–1. *Hypothetical distributions of organized and individualistic behaviors.* (Adapted from Allport, 3.)

of social control, adherence or conformity by members to some organizational rule or standard. It also illustrates one aspect of the order and predictability essential to organization: we know, or can predict within a relatively narrow margin of error, where a particular person is likely to fall on the scale if he is a member of a group whose behaviors distribute according to the solid-line curve. Most persons in this group fall within a very narrow range. In the case of the dashed-line curve, however, our prediction would be less certain and less reliable—as would an organization built on distributions of this kind.

Replaceability

Formal organization is set up to minimize—if not to eliminate—disruptions caused by personality and individual idiosyncrasy. It does not make a bit of difference from the point of view of formal organization *who* performs a given role, provided his behaviors are appropriate and conforming. It is often said that people come and go but the organization continues. This saying is true, because organizations are composed of *replaceable* members. Other, less formal types of social relationships, such as the family, do not have this facility. A mother, father, son, or daughter cannot be replaced readily, if at all.

Compensation

Members of work organizations are paid. They may receive perquisites in addition to pay, but money is usually considered a compensation for work. Generally, those who work harder or longer, or with greater skill, or who assume more responsibility in their work are paid more. The fact of pay is a basic fact of life for organizations, and it enters into some of the most serious problems which organizations face.

Technology

Another characteristic of work organizations is *technology*. Technology, whether it involves simple tools or massive assembly lines coordinated by complex computers, plays an integral role in shaping the character of the organization. Specialization, which we have already discussed, is one effect of technology. Technology also affects the physical proximity of persons and their opportunities to interact and form social groups (129). The large-scale introduction of automation in the factory and the office carries significant implications for the way in which formal organization must be designed and the way in which informal organization can develop. This is why the work organization is sometimes referred to as a *sociotechnical* system (45, 164).

Signs and Symbols

All formal organizations have symbols or signs of some kind to help identify the organization as a social entity or to facilitate discriminations within the organization itself. All formal organizations, for example, have names by which they are readily recognized: General Motors, U.S. Army, Acme Rubber Company, University of Michigan. Often associated with these titles are slogans, coats of arms, trade marks, and so forth, which help denote the organization and distinguish it from others. Titles, uniforms, badges, and insignia of various kinds generally appear within organizations. For instance, one man is called a press operator, another a manager; one wears a white shirt and tie, the other a blue shirt and overalls; one may have a stripe on his arm, the other a star on his shoulder; one has a mahogany desk and rug in his office, another (usually his subordinate) has a steel desk and no rug. Symbols also play a role in communications within the organization. In some organizations, the president has special stationery with the letterhead "From the office of the president." Special attention is given by subordinates to messages written on this stationery.

The signs and symbols that indicate rank or function in the organization, or that denote the organization itself, help to preserve the order and integrity of the total system. In the Army, for example, a private must be able to distinguish the sergeant from the captain at a glance. It is useful for clerks in the supermarket to be dressed in white so that customers can locate them easily and avoid annoying other customers when attempting to locate the beer counter. It also helps the manager to know at a glance where his clerks are in the otherwise confusing mass of persons on the floor.

Bureaucracy as a Model of Formal Organization

You have probably noticed that the role of the individual in the picture of organization that we have drawn is quite incidental—aside from the fact that he does the work. Members are more or less taken for granted. They are expendable, replaceable, interchangeable; they are expected to "fit" and not to get in the way of the grand design of the formal organization. There is little accounting in the picture for personality, for individual differences in value and attitude, for personal initiative, or for expressions of feelings or emotion. The elements of organization that we have described imply a *logical* or *rational* social system, and one must assume, if the system is to work according to plan, that the persons who make it up more or less adopt the organization's rationality as their own. These features of organization derive in large measure from attempts to meet the objective of efficiency.

The sociologist Max Weber coined the term *bureaucracy* as a label for a type of formal organization in which impersonality and rationality are developed to the highest degree. The term *bureaucracy* has since come to apply derogatorily to any kind of organizational inefficiency or waste, particularly in government. Bureaucracy as Weber conceived it, however, was to be the most efficient form of social organization, precisely because bureaucracy is coldly logical and because personalized relationships and nonrational, emotional considerations do not get in its way (173). The elements of the work organization which we have just described reflect, in a number of respects, the character of the bureaucratic organization.

Bureaucracy is a system of law, more than of man; a system in which rules cover all contingencies and where obedience is assured through the appointment of technically expert supervisors who administer law with precise and cold impartiality. The bureaucratic system is autocratic, since it has a rigid chain of command in which persons at the top give orders and those on the bottom unquestioningly obey. But the orders are always within the framework of the law. Obedience is never to the supervisor as a person and is therefore never based on personal affection (*charisma,* to use Weber's term), fear, or obligation; obedience is always to the abstract law, of which the supervisor is only an instrument. Members obey the law because it is their "duty," and because those who administer it are superior in technical knowledge. Alfred Krupp, the well-known German industrialist, epitomized some of the spirit of this model in expressing his administrative aspirations for the mammoth Krupp Steel Works: "What I shall attempt to bring about is that nothing of importance shall happen or be caused to happen without the foreknowledge and approval of the management; that the past and the determinable future of the establishment can be learned in the files of the management without asking a question of any mortal" (quoted from 115, in 17, p. 6).

Robert Merton describes some of the requirements of bureaucracy as follows:

> If bureaucracy is to operate successfully, it must attain a high degree of reliability of behavior, an unusual degree of conformity with prescribed patterns of action. Hence, the fundamental importance of discipline . . . [which] can be effective only if the ideal patterns are buttressed by strong sentiments which entail devotion to one's duties, a keen sense of the limitation of one's authority and competence, and methodical performance of routine activities (108, p. 365).

The bureaucratic model may not seem so severe when compared with some other types of organizations. More "personalized" organization is illustrated in many organizations of primitive societies, in feudalism, and in the family-type business where leadership is inherited. In some of these more traditional organizations, the subordinate owes allegiance to the superior as a servant does a master. Obedience is demanded as a personal service in many areas of life—not just within the narrowly defined limits of the job. Superiors can exercise arbitrary power based on whim or personal taste, practicing nepotism or exhibiting favoritism toward those they like while discriminating against those who are disfavored. Bureaucracy, on the other hand, defines the rules of the game so as to restrict the prerogatives of the superior within legitimate, job-essential bounds, guaranteeing equal treatment for all subordinates. Rational and objective criteria, such as seniority or tested competence—not personal preference by the superior—are, theoretically, the bases for advancement.

The rationality and impersonality of the bureaucratic model can be seen partly as a protection for the member against arbitrary and abusive rule, a way of making his life in the organization more predictable and stable and less dependent on the personal whim of an arbitrary leader. In turn, the member is expected to do his duty. The end result, according to Weber, is extremely felicitous:

> Experience tends universally to show that the purely bureaucratic type of administrative organization . . . is, from a purely technical point of view, capable of attaining the highest degree of efficiency and is in this sense formally the most rational known means of carrying out imperative control over human beings. It is superior to any other form in precision, in stability, in the stringency of its discipline, and in its reliabilty (172, p. 337).

Needless to say, the bureaucratic model of formal organization is rarely found in pure form. Weber saw resemblances to it in the up-to-date military organizations of his day (early twentieth century) and in the Catholic Church. He also saw it as applicable to most large-scale industrial organizations. A number of contemporary sociological theorists have elaborated and modified Weber's ideas so as to make them more applicable to modern organization (25, 38, 58, 138). Nevertheless, Weber's original insights stand today among the most important contributions to our understanding of organizations.

Administrative Models of Formal Organization

The Weberian model of bureaucracy was developed largely out of an academic and theoretical interest in organizations. Administrative scientists who were more closely committed to the development of guidelines for organizational practice adopted their own approach to the problem of organizing human effort in the most efficient way possible. The classical theories developed by administrative scientists shared with

Weber's bureaucracy the elements of rationality and the consequent relegation of individual personality to a secondary theoretical role.

Administrative approaches are concerned in part with the construction of a rational or optimal system of task allocations. March and Simon refer to these systems of allocations as *theories of departmentalization* and provide the following summary description:

> Given a general purpose for an organization, we can identify the unit tasks necessary to achieve that purpose. These tasks will normally include basic productive activities, service activities, coordinative activities, supervisory activities, etc. The problem is to group these tasks into individual jobs, to group the jobs into administrative units, to group the units into larger units, and finally to establish the top-level departments—and to make these groupings in such a way as to minimize the total cost of carrying out all the activities (104, p. 22).

The allocation of tasks is a *structural* problem, and it has led to a consideration of several dimensions of organization which help define its "shape" (120):

1. *Flatness and tallness* illustrate one such dimension. This dimension refers to the number of hierarchical levels in the organization. The Sears Roebuck Company, for example, is unusually flat for its size, with only four levels intervening between the rank-and-file employees and the president. The Catholic Church, too, is a relatively flat organization, with only a few levels of hierarchy between the priest and the Pope. Most large companies are likely to have relatively tall structures, with about a dozen or more levels between the bottom and top. Army ranking also illustrates a tall structure; privates, at the bottom, are a long way from the commander in chief, at the top.

2. *Span of control,* another feature of hierarchy, has been much discussed in the administrative literature. This term refers simply to the number of subordinates who report to a single supervisor. Administrative experts have debated the relative effectiveness of different spans of control, with some arguing that the span should not exceed three and others arguing for a span as great as twenty.

3. *Line and staff* are distinguished often in discussions of administrative structure. The *line* refers to the organizational chain of command concerned directly with the production process for which the or-

ganization is manifestly created. The *staff* is indirect and auxiliary in its function. It aids the top executive and enlarges his ability to co-ordinate by providing expert advice or other administrative services. The need for the staff function derives from the complexity of the large organization and the technical expertise which is necessary in running it.

To the administrator, then, is given the responsibility of designing the organization in the terms we have discussed. Individual differences, motivation, and personality do not play much of a role in this conception of formal organization, although the administrative literature cautions that some human difficulties will arise in the ideal plan and that there will be a need for minor adjustments. But, for the classical administrative theorist as for the bureaucratic, such adjustments are expected to be only temporary exceptions from the grand design. In fact these excep-tions often turn out to be more important than the rule, as we shall see.

chapter two

The Human Factor
in Organization

The bureaucratic and administrative theories discussed in the pre-ceding chapter are eminently unpsychological in that they pay little at-tention to individual motivation. In principle, they recognize *esprit de corps* and *morale,* as general motivational forces, but they do not explore these forces in detail. However, near the turn of the century, F. W. Taylor (162) helped launch a movement called *scientific management.* This movement has had a significant impact on organizational practice, and the principles upon which it is based contrast with those of bureau-cratic and administrative theory in that scientific management pays greater attention to the organization member, to the details of his work behavior, and to his job motivation.

Scientific Management

Certain crucial aspects of Taylor's approach are consistent with the spirit of bureaucratic and administrative theory: Taylor, too, wanted to create a rational organization. Although his attention focused on in-dividual workers and their jobs, he proposed to "systematize" the opera-tions of the plant. In describing the kind of organization he hoped to achieve, Taylor stressed several characteristics of the formal work or-ganization:

1. Efficiency. (Like the bureaucratic and administrative theories, Taylor's system was addressed to the objective of efficiency—or, as he once put it more concretely, "to stop the loafing."[1])

[1] This and the following quotes are taken from a letter written by Taylor in 1898 to the president of the Bethlehem Iron Company. Reprinted in Copley (37), pp. 10–13.

2. Standardization of job performance and the uniformity of behavior that standardization implies. (Each workman was to be instructed as to the best, scientifically determined method for performing a job "instead of leaving it to each individual's judgment." Among the advantages of standardization are impersonalization and replaceability, which permit the running of a shop "entirely independent of any one man or any set of men.")

3. Discipline and hierarchical authority. (Taylor's system was to be such "that any policy which may be decided upon by the management can be properly carried out.")

In this context, it is not surprising that Taylor recommended such bureaucratic principles as the selection of workers on the basis of fitness for the job rather than on the basis of friendship or personal influence, and written rather than verbal instructions: "Otherwise, the responsibility for an error cannot be properly located." But his main interest was in two aspects of the scientific-management program: (a) using workers' energies efficiently; and (b) motivating workers to produce rapidly.

Efficient Use of Energy

Taylor was concerned primarily with workers who performed routine tasks. He noted that such workers' movements are similar to those of a machine. These movements could therefore be planned so as to involve the most efficient and least fatiguing use of energy. As a result of suggestions by Taylor and his colleagues, *time-and-motion* experts were trained to study a job in order to discover "the one best way" of doing it (55). The tools of the trade included the stopwatch and a set of principles of motion economy. A number of such principles have evolved over the years. For example:[2]

1. "Smooth, continuous motions of the hands are preferable to zig-zag motions or straight-line motions involving sudden and sharp changes in direction."

[2] The following quotes are from R. M. Barnes, *Motion and Time Study* (New York, 1949), summarized in March and Simon (104), p. 20.

2. "Motions of the arms should be made in opposite and symmetrical directions and should be made simultaneously."

3. "The two hands should begin as well as complete their motions at the same time."

Besides specifying the motions of a job, scientific-management principles have been developed to cover the design of tools and equipment and the arrangement of the workplace for most efficient work performance. Scientific management has been concerned with such things as the height of work benches and chairs, the shape and placement of tools, illumination, and length of rest pauses.

Motivating Workers

A second aspect of the scientific-management approach is the motivation of employees to work as rapidly as possible while employing "the one best way." Taylor proposed the *piecework incentive system of pay* as an answer to the problem of motivation: that is, the more pieces a man produces, the greater his pay. Taylor relates a story—a classic in the development of scientific management—to illustrate his approach: In 1898 he was hired by the Bethlehem Iron Company (which later became part of the Bethlehem Steel Corporation) to introduce more efficient work methods. One of his tasks was to improve the work of pig-iron handlers—gangs of men who loaded 92-pound pigs onto a railroad car. Taylor was warned that these men, who handled about 12½ tons of iron per day, "were steady workers, but slow and phlegmatic, and that nothing would induce them to work fast" (162, p. 48). Undaunted, Taylor studied the job of pig handling and concluded that with proper, less fatiguing methods, first-class workers could handle 47 or 48 tons a day—about four times the average. In order to introduce his method, Taylor selected a "little Pennsylvania Dutchman," fictitiously called Schmidt, who he felt would be receptive to his approach:

> The task before us, then, narrowed itself down to getting Schmidt to handle 47 tons of pig iron per day and making him glad to do it. This was done as follows. Schmidt was called out from among the gang of pig-iron handlers and talked to somewhat this way:
> "Schmidt, are you a high-priced man?" . . .
> "Vell, I don't know vat you mean."

"Oh, come now, you answer my questions. What I want to find out is whether you are a high-priced man or one of these cheap fellows here. What I want to find out is whether you want to earn $1.85 a day or whether you are satisfied with $1.15, just the same as all those cheap fellows are getting."

"Did I vant $1.85 a day? Vas dot a high-priced man? Vell, yes, I vas a high-priced man."

". . . Now come over here. You see that pile of pig iron?"

"Yes."

"You see that car?"

"Yes."

"Well, if you are a high-priced man, you will load that pig iron on that car tomorrow for $1.85. Now do wake up and answer my question. Tell me whether you are a high-priced man or not."

"Vell—did I got $1.85 for loading dot pig iron on dot car tomorrow?" . . .

"Certainly you do—certainly you do."

"Vell, den, I vas a high-priced man."

"Now, hold on, hold on. You know just as well as I do that a high-priced man has to do exactly as he's told from morning till night. You have seen this man here before, haven't you?"

"No, I never saw him."

"Well, if you are a high-priced man, you will do exactly as this man tells you tomorrow, from morning till night. When he tells you to pick up a pig and walk, you pick it up and you walk, and when he tells you to sit down and rest, you sit down. You do that right straight through the day. And what's more, no back talk. Do you understand that? When this man tells you to walk, you walk; when he tells you to sit down, you sit down, and you don't talk back at him. Now you come on to work here tomorrow morning and I'll know before night whether you are really a high-priced man or not."[3]

So Schmidt loaded the car as instructed, earned $1.85, and illustrated the efficacy of Taylor's method.

[3] Frederick Winslow Taylor, *Scientific Management*, pp. 44–46. Copyright 1911 by Frederick W. Taylor; copyright renewed 1939 by Louise M. S. Taylor. Reprinted with the permission of Harper & Row, Publishers.

Some Questions about Scientific Management

It is not surprising that Taylor came under attack from various quarters for his treatment of Schmidt and for the ethics his approach seemed to imply. A young socialist named Upton Sinclair, for example, wondered why Taylor "gave about 61 per cent increase in wages, and got 362 per cent increase in work" (37, pp. 50–55). Labor unions, too, in this country and abroad, raised objections to scientific management, which they asserted was a device for exploiting workers (54, pp. 261–290). Ironically, one source of opposition to Taylor's efforts in the Bethlehem Company was the owners. When they saw that Taylor was cutting their labor force to about one fourth of its previous size, they were faced with the unhappy realization that he was depopulating South Bethlehem, where they owned all of the houses and the company stores. When Taylor reminded them, in the face of these objections, that this was precisely what he had said at the outset he would do, they replied that they hadn't believed then that he could do it (37, p. 46).

Despite opposition, scientific management has been adopted in industrial circles throughout the world. In recent years even many labor unions have accepted the principles of scientific management, including time-and-motion study and piecework. The application of these principles has been tempered, however, so that the Schmidt case seems a slightly embarrassing anachronism. Some unions even employ experts trained in scientific-management principles. These experts are available to help managements devise more efficient and less costly work methods (18, p. 111).

In spirit scientific management, in its cold rationality, resembles the classical bureaucratic and administrative theories. The conception of man is not far from that of an automaton whose performance can be improved through the application of logical engineering principles and simple economic incentives. Taylor developed what appeared to be a *logically* unbeatable combination: efficient motions, efficient tools, optimum working arrangements, together with strong incentives. Yet scientific management did not always work—for the same reason that the classical approaches to organization did not always work. The problem was the *human factor*—that complex, elusive, emotional, social, and sometimes nonrational being whose behaviors comprise the substance of the organization. The classical approaches either ignored the human factor or oversimplified it. A significant point of departure in this growing realization was the famous Hawthorne research, which was designed within the framework of scientific management but which led off in a new direction, into a new movement called *human relations*.

The Hawthorne Studies

Horace Walpole refers to the story of three princes from the kingdom of Serendip who set out in quest of an object. The princes sought far and wide but did not find what they were looking for; on the way, however, they discovered many interesting things, which proved to be more important than the original object of their search. Walpole coined the term *serendipity*, in honor of the three princes of Serendip, to describe the general process of discovering one thing while looking for something else.

Scientific discovery is often a matter of serendipity, as the Hawthorne studies illustrate. These studies were launched during 1924 in the Hawthorne Works of the Western Electric Company, and their surprising and dramatic results rocked the foundations of traditional management theory. The experiments spanned about a decade, but well before they were through, the experimenters began to discover some things of an order quite different from what they had expected. Among these things was the power of the *informal* organization. Let us see how these discoveries occurred (71, Chs. 3–6, 86, 124, 165).

The Illumination Experiments

The first group of experiments in the series, carried out in collaboration with the National Research Council, was concerned with the effects of illumination on worker productivity. Although these experiments were preliminary to the main body of the Hawthorne research, they are important in that they set the stage for the studies that followed. The illumination experiments were conducted in several departments employing female workers engaged in winding coils, assembling relays, and inspecting small parts. The experimenters varied the conditions of light intensity under which the operators worked, fully expecting the workers' output to vary systematically with candle power. The early results showed no such effect; productivity varied erratically as illumination increased. As the experiment proceeded, the results became increasingly mystifying: two groups within a single department—a control group working under constant conditions of light and a test group under increasing light intensity—showed equal and substantial increases in productivity.

The problem, the experimenters thought, must be a contamination due to the mixture of artificial and natural light. They attempted, therefore, to refine the experimental conditions by eliminating natural light; but the effect was no more satisfying. Productivity again increased at a steady pace in both a control group, where light intensity was held constant, and in a test group, where it was *decreased*. As a matter of fact, employees continued to produce efficiently until light intensity was reduced to the very uncomfortable level of 3 foot-candles; and one group of volunteer girls, in a further informal experiment, maintained a high level of productivity under conditions approximating ordinary moonlight! Paradoxically, members of this group reported "that they suffered no eyestrain and that they became less tired than when working under bright lights" (124, p. 17). As one experimenter put it, "A literal interpretation of the results would have suggested that poor illumination is desirable, for a comparison of two comparable groups of workers showed that those working with gradually reduced illumination had a higher output than those with ideal illumination. Such a conclusion would be obviously absurd" (165, p. 578).

At the end of this first group of experiments, it became apparent that within very wide limits, illumination as a physical characteristic of the work environment had no predictable effect on worker productivity. Something else must have been behind the improved performance of the girls.

The Relay-Assembly Test Room

A second group of experiments, launched in 1927, was conducted in collaboration with researchers from the Harvard School of Business Administration (as were the remaining parts of the Hawthorne studies). This group of experiments was designed to investigate the effects of working conditions, such as length of rest pauses and length of working days, on workers' performance. It seemed self-evident that such effects should exist, and the researchers had little doubt when these studies were initiated that, within a year or less, definite answers to their questions could be obtained. "But," as Roethlisberger and Dickson explained in their comprehensive report, "the inquiry developed in an unexpected fashion" (124, p. 3).

In this experiment, the researchers attempted to control more precisely than in the illumination study some of the physical conditions that might affect work performance. They set up a test room where they could take careful measurements of room temperature and humidity, and they recorded the amount of sleep the workers had had the previous night. The girls were also given medical checkups about every six weeks, since physical health was considered an important variable. Finally, the experimenters placed an observer in the test room. His functions were "(1) to keep accurate records of all that happened, and (2) to create and maintain a friendly amosphere in the test room" (124, p. 22).

Six girls were placed in the test room, five of them to assemble small relays as they had been doing in their own departments and another to act as a layout operator.

For two years, the relay-assembly experiment went through thirteen periods, with each period differing from the previous one in length or frequency of rest pauses or in length of workweek.

The experimenters evaluated the results after the first seven periods —a part of the experiment that was concerned primarily with variations in rest pauses. Table 2–1 defines the experimental conditions during these periods; and the left-hand portion of Figure 2–1 shows the average productivity of the operators during this phase of the experiment. The

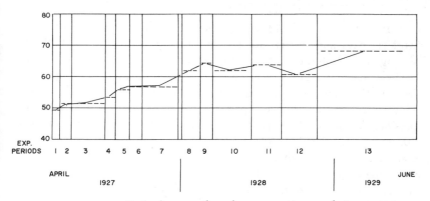

FIGURE 2–1. *Average hourly output per week in the relay-assembly test room.* (Adapted from 124, p. 76.)

curve of productivity follows a general upward trend. Since the amount of time given to rest pauses increased from periods 4 through 7, as Table 2–1 shows, the improvement in rate of output was attributed to these pauses. The increase in period 3, in advance of the introduction of rest pauses, was explained by a special group-pay incentive that was introduced (and maintained throughout the experiment). These results appeared to be about what one would expect within the scientific-management framework.

TABLE 2–1. *Experimental conditions during periods 1–7 in the relay-assembly test room.* (From 124, p. 57.)

PERIOD	LENGTH IN WEEKS	EXPERIMENTAL CONDITIONS OF WORK
1	2	Standard
2	5	Standard
3	8	Standard
4	5	Two 5 min. rests
5	4	Two 10 min. rests
6	4	Six 5 min. rests
7	11	15 min. A.M. rest and lunch; 10 min. P.M. rest

Periods 8 through 13 were concerned primarily with lengths of working days and weeks, but the experimenters decided to duplicate during several of these periods the experimental conditions of earlier periods (see Table 2–2). Again a general trend of increasing productivity was observed (as indicated in the right-hand portion of Fig. 2–1). However, some revealing comparisons could be made which were not possible during the first half of this experiment. For instance, period 10, which was an exact replication of period 7 in terms of experimental conditions, was nevertheless superior to 7 in productivity. Period 13 was superior both to 10 and 7, which it otherwise duplicated; and 12 was clearly superior to the earlier "standard" period that it otherwise reproduced. The generally increasing productivity during this experiment resembled some of the strange effects of the earlier experiments; that is the results suggested that something in the experiments considerably more potent than the length of rest pauses or workweeks had influenced the output of the operators.[4]

TABLE 2–2. *Experimental conditions during periods 8–13 in the relay-assembly test room.* (From 124, p. 77.)

PERIOD	LENGTH IN WEEKS	EXPERIMENTAL CONDITIONS OF WORK
8	7	Same as 7, but 4:30 stop
9	4	Same as 7, but 4:00 stop
10	12	Same as 7
11	9	Same as 7, but Sat. A.M. off
12	12	Standard
13	31	Same as 7

In their report of the experiment, Roethlisberger and Dickson considered retrospectively what had happened:

> In looking back, it is clear that two essentially different sorts of changes occurred in the first seven periods of the experiment. There were those changes introduced by the investigators in the form of experimental conditions; these were well noted and recorded. There was another type of change, however, of which the investigators were not so consciously aware. . . . From [the] attempt to set the proper conditions for the experiment, there arose indirectly a change in human relations which came to be of great significance in the next stage of the experiment, when it became necessary to seek a new hypothesis to explain certain unexpected results of the inquiry (124, pp. 58–59).

The elements of "human relations" that distinguished the test room from the regular work department can be summarized under four related headings:

[4] At the end of period 7, two girls were replaced in the experiment. Part of the increase during period 8 may therefore be attributed to the new personnel. However, the remaining girls also increased their productivity, so the general upward trend is not due simply to the replacements.

SUPERVISORY STYLE

Supervision in the test room was largely in the hands of the test-room observer and the other experimenters, who were trying to create and maintain a friendly atmosphere so that the experimental changes, such as the rest pauses, would be accepted without difficulty. Supervision was therefore less stringent and restrictive than usual. For example, the girls were permitted to talk more freely, and the observer-supervisor, in trying to dispel apprehensions about the test, conversed in an easy and informal manner with them, sometimes about personal matters or their attitudes toward the test. The supervisors' behavior, together with the health examinations, luncheons, and occasional birthday parties (for which the company shared the expenses), created an atmosphere in which the girls were given a great deal of considerate and personal attention. In sum, the experimental supervision was more friendly, attentive, and personally interested, and less restrictive, coercive, and punitive than the regular supervision.

CONTROL

Not only were the girls under less stringent control while in the test room, they were even allowed to exercise some control over their work—a prerogative not granted them in the regular departments. This liberty developed out of the experimenters' sensitivity to the girls' feelings and wishes. Under certain circumstances, the girls could even veto proposals of the experimenters. For example, the investigators at one point decided to change the method of paying the girls without changing the amount of their pay. When the girls expressed strong opposition to the change (because of their "irrational" suspicion that management was contriving to do them out of their earnings), the experimenters quickly withdrew the proposal. Thus, the girls participated—sometimes explicitly, sometimes implicitly—in the decision-making processes that affected their lives in the workplace.

GROUP FORMATION

The factor that the girls felt contributed most to the high productivity in the test room was *the small group*. Roethlisberger and Dickson described the development of a cohesive group structure as follows:

> No longer were the girls isolated individuals, working together only in the sense of an actual physical proximity.

They had become participating members of a working group with all the psychological and social implications peculiar to such a group. In period 10, a growing amount of social activity developed among the test-room girls outside of working hours and outside of the plant. The conversation in the test room became more socialized. In period 13, the girls began to help one another out for the common good of the group. They had became bound together by common sentiments and feelings of loyalty (124, p. 86).

The kinds of affectional ties that bound the girls into a tight-knit group, and the cooperative efforts that grew out of this can be seen in the following record of the observer (124, p. 74):

April 19, 1929, . . . after the observer told the operators what their percentage for the previous day had been, the following conversation took place:

Operator 5: "I made it." (Referring to the percentage.)

Operator 4: "Say, Operator 1 and I made your percentage for you yesterday."

Operator 2: "I guess we all made it for Operator 5 yesterday. I can't understand, I'm working so hard today and I can't make as much as yesterday."

Operator 3: "I'm about 15 relays behind yesterday."

Operator 2: "Oh, don't say that! Don't you work according to the way you feel?"

Operator 3: "Do you?"

Operator 2: "I always do! Do you feel like working?"

Operator 3: "Sure, and how!"

Operator 2: "Well, go ahead, because I don't."

Operator 4: (to Operator 2) "Don't worry about your percentage. Operator 1 and I will make it for you."

Operator 5: "I made 421 yesterday and I'm going to make better today."

Operator 2: "That's fine."

Not only did the girls cooperate in their work, and encourage each other to do well, but they might also put pressure on one of the slower girls:

Operator 1: "We had better stop razzing Operator 3 and we will always have a high percentage."

Operator 2:   "What happened with her that she put out so many relays? Gee! That's the first time she was working so hard."

Operator 4:   "I know why. Because we didn't razz her all day."

Operator 3:   "Don't bother me because I won't make any percentage if you do."

MORALE

Very much related to each of the above characteristics of the experiment was the generally heightened sense of satisfaction the girls experienced in the test room. As one of the girls put it, "it was fun." The girls liked the test room and they enjoyed their work more there than in the department. Work in the test room had an intrinsic psychological payoff—no doubt because of the special attention, the less restrictive supervision, the control which the girls could exercise over some of the things that affected them, and the affectional ties in the small group. The girls earned more money because of their higher productivity, no doubt another source of satisfaction, and they felt they were part of something important. Psychologically speaking, the girls were *ego involved*.

Informal Organization

In terms of classical conceptions of formal organization, the events in the test room are hardly recognizable. Nor do the principles of scientific management help explain the maverick organization that evolved. The formal organization plan, along with its traditional style of discipline and hierarchical control, was seriously compromised. The reactions of the girls to each other and to the supervisor were anything but impersonal, and the supervisor was not entirely indifferent or unresponsive to the feelings of his subordinates. Furthermore, the girls were active rather than passive elements in the organization. It was clear that they were acting as much in terms of individual tastes and personal needs as in terms of formal organizational requirements. Thus personality, emotion, and sentiment played important roles—contrary to the formal organization ideal. The test-room system was characterized by more spontaneity, and even by more idiosyncratic behavior, than is usually considered respectable.

Yet the organization in the test room was extremely effective. Production increased an average of 30 per cent. Some of the girls were so highly motivated that they often did not realize how hard they were working. While discipline in the traditional sense was reduced to a minimum, significant control was exercised through the informal social system that evolved. For one thing, the group informally adopted a leader (Operator 2). But the girls themselves also exercised control over each other through mutual encouragement or through pressures against a deviant low producer. Mutual influences extended throughout the group so that each member could count on the others' help when it was needed, and each was prepared in turn to help the others. The outcome was a highly motivated and cooperative group of workers.

The events of the test room illustrate some of the important elements of informal organization: (a) the spontaneous unplanned development of stable relationships based on personal attraction or mutual dependency; (b) the development of standards of acceptable behavior (for example, high productivity or mutual help); and (c) the enforcement of these standards by an informal leader (for example, Operator 2), or by peers (for example, by razzing a low producer).

Informal organization, however, does not require experimental test rooms. Later phases of the Hawthorne research and studies in other organizations have helped document the universality and importance of informal organization intertwined with the formal. The test room was unique only in that it created a group with standards of production so outstandingly high. Informal organization can also work to restrict productivity, as later phases of the Hawthorne research demonstrated. We shall consider this phenomenon in Chapter 5. But, for better or for worse, the Hawthorne test room revealed a social psychology of the work organization which, to those concerned with problems of organizational performance, seemed to hold within it a force of revolutionary power.

chapter three

The Individual in the Organization

The classical views of organization either ignore the individual or they make oversimplified assumptions about him. A result of this oversight is the breach between theory and practice in organizations, between the way organizations *should* work and the way they *do* work. For instance, informal organization (which stems in part from the personal needs and interpersonal relationships of members) is not accounted for in the formal plan. The Hawthorne research scientifically documented this important human aspect of organization and made it patently clear that psychological or social psychological principles of behavior were at work in the test room. The research also showed that organization theory would somehow have to take these principles into account. Let us look briefly at some of the psychological and social psychological principles which are relevant to the adjustments of members and to their performance in the organization.

Personality

"The outstanding characteristic of man," according to Gordon W. Allport, "is his individuality" (6, p. 3). The concept of personality helps denote some of the important individuality of people. Several aspects of personality are especially pertinent to man's behavior in organizations. First, personality is relatively *stable*. It is formed during the early years of growth—infancy and childhood. Once formed, however, the adult personality does not change readily. The individual therefore comes to the organization with his personality pretty much as a "given."

Second, personality characteristics are said to be *general*. This means simply that an individual tries to express his distinctive personality in a variety of situations. He does not leave his personality at the gate when he enters an organizational role. Third, personality is *motivational*; it implies strivings, wants, needs, or "determining tendencies." Characteristics of personality are not simply ways of classifying or typing people, but, more dynamically, they tell us something about what the individual is *characteristically trying to do,* consciously or unconsciously (5).

Motives Relevant to the Adjustments of Organization Members

Specific motives that are important in the adjustment of large numbers of people are often considered *personality needs*. They are formed during early stages of psychological development and are assumed to remain fairly stable, although they may be aroused by situational factors. We shall discuss several of these motives which are especially relevant to the adjustments of people in the work organization.

Need for Affiliation

Men seek the company of others. This tendency toward social contact has led some psychologists to postulate a kind of herd instinct, sometimes called *gregariousness*. However, few psychologists today give much credence to instinct as an explanation for behavior; more likely, the need for affiliation develops through the dependency relationship between the child and his parents.

Whatever the explanation for its development, the need for social contact is highly potent in many people. Impressive evidence for its importance comes through the experience of individuals who have lived in isolation as hermits or prisoners—or as subjects in the psychological laboratory. Extended isolation can be extremely painful for some, and its continued effects may even lead to a mental state approaching insanity.

Experiments by Schachter and others have been very helpful in elucidating some of the conditions under which the affiliation motive may be most highly aroused (14, 128, 131, 141). A threat that produces fear seems to be one such condition. Frustration, such as that resulting from the missing of several meals, is another. Persons are more likely to seek each other's company under these conditions than when they are not threatened or frustrated. Furthermore, they appear to seek persons who are experiencing the same adversity. The presence of others seems to alleviate some of the anxiety. This phenomenon can be understood partly in terms of the affection, love, sympathy, or sense of succorance that may accompany affiliative behavior (22). There is little room for these sentiments, however, in the formal organization. Yet they are present where there are people, and they form an important motivational basis for the informal organization.

Ego-Relevant Motives

Under this heading fall a number of motives that imply something about a person's self-identity. Individuals are generally motivated to achieve and maintain a favorable self-concept. They want to think well of themselves; to have, in Maslow's terms, *self-respect* or *self-esteem* (107, 111). In general, reactions of others which imply approval, acceptance, respect, recognition, attention, or appreciation, or which attribute importance or worth to an individual, bring some sense of ego enhancement. Status and prestige or other indications of success are also sought as a means of assuring a favorable self-identity. Satisfaction of the need for esteem is accompanied, according to Maslow, by feelings of adequacy, well-being, and confidence. Frustration of these needs leads to a sense of inferiority, weakness, and helplessness, and, under certain circumstances, to neurosis (51, 77, 107).

Skills, talents, and abilities are often associated with an individual's self-identity. These abilities are not in themselves sources of motivation (although they are intimately connected with the personality and with other needs); rather, they represent potentials or capabilities that individuals want to fulfill. The terms *self-actualization* and *self-fulfillment* are sometimes used to describe this need in people to employ their skills, and realize whatever their potentialities may be.

Power Motives

People have feelings, sometimes intense, about power—about controlling others and being controlled by others. Since power in social situations is often considered a mark of status or of success, it may be sought to satisfy these goals. The power relationship may also be associated with feelings of superiority or inferiority, with a sense of dominance or submission, or with independence or dependence. It may even imply, as some psychoanalytical writers argue, something about manliness and virility. Attitudes toward power, therefore, are emotionally charged and are closely related to ego motives.

Psychologists have investigated the tendencies of individuals to be dependent or independent, or to control or be controlled, and have developed tests to measure authoritarianism, egalitarianism, the need for independence, and the need for power (2, 167). These measures relate significantly to conformity behavior and to other reactions of persons to authority (39, 157, 168).

Curiosity

Man's curiosity leads him to seek, explore, wonder, investigate, or to manipulate many aspects of his environment. The curiosity motive is most likely to find opportunity for expression where the environment of the individual is complex, strange, novel, varied, or surprising (21). But man is not the only animal motivated by pure curiosity—or subject to disinterest in environmental objects which are familiar and constant. Chimpanzees also have the urge to explore, and they too can become bored with an object that once attracted keen interest (174).

Security

By *security* we mean a state in which most of the important needs of a person can be satisfied and in which the individual is reasonably assured of their continued satisfaction. *Insecurity* implies apprehension or anxiety about the maintenance of these satisfactions, and may be associated with economic, social, or psychological factors. Persons who fear the loss of a job or steady income, or are in doubt about their ability to meet their bills, to achieve their aspirations, or to maintain friendships or other relationships that are important to them are likely to suffer a sense of insecurity. Insecurity may be *situational;* for example, it may result from a failure caused by adverse circumstances. Or it may be a more permanent function of personality; some people are insecure even though they are successful by all outward standards. Insecurity is a distressing and sometimes debilitating emotion.

Emotion

Psychologists sometimes speak of emotion as a source of motivation. Roller coasters and frightening movies provide some gratification for the need to experience emotion. Persons who feel emotions such as fear, anger, joy, elation, exuberance, rage, and hate do not remain im-passive. They are likely to *express* their feelings through their facial expressions or their tone of voice, or through laughing, crying, or other forms of cathartic behavior. Emotion is animating; it leads to action, and, in this sense at least, it is motivational.

Emotion also *accompanies* behavior and may be recognized in the *intensity* with which a person behaves: for instance, a man runs faster, works harder, and perseveres longer when "spurred" by emotion. The satisfaction or the frustration of needs may evoke emotion. Frustration sometimes leads to anger or hate and consequently to forms of aggres-sive behavior. On the other hand, the disposition toward persons who are the source of satisfaction is likely to be favorable, including perhaps the emotions of love and affection. These emotions underlie some forms of affiliation.

Economic Motivation

As an incentive, money is frequently associated with the "economic-man" concept, which has played an important role in the development of economic theory. This conception of human nature was introduced by Adam Smith and makes two major assumptions: (a) that man is perfectly rational; and (b) that he is guided by an exclusive desire to maximize his money position. Scientific management relied on this view in stressing the value of piece-rate incentives.

The economic-man concept, however, is a gross oversimplification (78). It is inconsistent with most of the precepts of personality and motivation that we have just described, since it implies that all men are more or less alike; are simple, unemotional, and uninterested in any-thing but money; and are able to calculate profits and losses and debits and assets with unerring accuracy.

In rejecting the economic-man concept, however, an important caution should be exercised. Money is an important incentive in our society—even though the economic man concept does not help us to understand how or why people react to it. People want money; they want to save it, spend it, or show it. They need it to buy the things that are essential to life—food, clothing, and shelter—and they need it to ac-quire the luxuries that are also essential to life (or seem to be, in an "affluent society" of ascending aspirations). Through effective advertis-ing, business and industrial organizations help create a rising spiral of consumer needs, which contributes to the demand for material goods.

Money is important because it buys things that people value, but the importance of money is as much psychological as it is economic. "It is clear," William James put it, "that between what a man calls *me* and what he simply calls *mine* is a line difficult to draw" (74). A man's wages are part of his self-identity. In general, money seems to be among the most prominent sources of worry for contemporary Americans according to a nationwide survey by Gurin, Veroff, and Feld (61, pp. 25–26):

> Economic and material matters . . . figure importantly in the sense of happiness and unhappiness which Americans experience. Contrary to the tendency of the romantic to depreciate the importance of money for happiness, people attach primary importance to economic and material considerations as they think about happiness and unhappiness. . . . Happiness is expressed in terms of having "enough" money, being free from debt, having a "nice" home. . . . Similarly, the complaints . . . refer to such things as debts, bills, and inadequate housing.[1]

Implications of Motivation for Adjustment in the Organization

Motivation, by definition, affects behavior. A person's motivational state also affects how he perceives the world, and how he interprets what he perceives (95, pp. 85–116). In the realm of interpersonal relations, the perception by one person of another is colored by the relationship between them—whether, for example, the relationship is a source of need fulfillment or one of frustration. Supervisors, therefore, do not view their subordinates with complete neutrality or objectivity—any more than subordinates regard their supervisors in this coldly rational way. Perceptions between people in organizations, between supervisors and subordinates, or between peers, are highly *personalized*. This psychological principle represents another blow to the rational "economic-man" concept. Nonrational, motivational forces affect, if not distort, the perceptions of the very facts upon which the "rational" man bases his "logical" plan of action.

[1] See also Stuhr (152) and Herzberg et al. (70) for illustrations of the importance some workers attach to wages.

The qualities of personality and motivation that we have discussed are inconsistent with the requirements of formal organization. The human organism lacks the rationality, simplicity, and passivity that classical organization theories assume it has. People are complex, varied, and animated. They have needs, sometimes deeply felt, long before they come to the organization—and they do not give up these needs when they join. Individuals are therefore motivated in ways that, from the point of "the system," are quite extraneous. People are "driven" to express their unique personalities, to gain approval, to achieve status, to experience sentiment or emotion, to acquire wealth, to give and receive affection, to enhance their egos, to "actualize" their potentialities, to avoid insecurity, and to satisfy other basic motives—all of which are interrelated in complex ways. These motives help define what we might call a person's self-interest. However, the formal work organization is not ordinarily designed with the members' self-interest in mind. The organization has quite another purpose—and herein lies a conflict of serious proportions, as we shall see in the next chapter.

chapter four

Personal Adjustment and Conflict in the Work Organization

Man versus Organization

The conflict between man and organization has interested social philosophers for some time. One of the historical roots of this interest can be traced to Rousseau, who saw in institutionalization the destruction of man's true and better nature. Karl Marx and a number of other sociological theorists have written about the frustrations imposed on man by the nature of industrial organization. The conflict lies partly in the specialization and routinization of mass production and partly in the worker's lack of control over his work or over his destiny in the organization. According to Marx, the worker is "separated" from the means of production, which he does not own, and suffers "alienation"—a sense of powerlessness and a lack of positive identity with his work (106, 135).

Contemporary social critics also have been concerned with the relationship of man to the organization in which he works. The term *organization man* has become common parlance since Whyte's "exposé" of the pressures for conformity among middle-level executives. These executives not only work for the organization, they *belong* to it. "They are the ones of our middle class who have left home, spiritually as well as physically, to take the vows of organization life, and it is they who are the mind and soul of our great self-perpetuating institutions" (177, p. 3). The pressures toward conformity in organizations have been portrayed in the extreme through the fiction of Huxley and of Orwell. "Round pegs in square holes," as Huxley puts it, "tend to have dangerous thoughts about the social system and to infect others with their discontent" (73, p. xvi). Although the analogy lacks subtlety, one might

33

say that the formal organization *does* imply square holes, and *some* people, at least, are round.

The issue of man versus organization was posed for psychologists a number of years ago by F. H. Allport, who stressed the importance of individual differences in the personal characteristics of organization members.

> There are many individuals having degrees of [a] trait which cannot be expressed if the individual is to act in obedience to the institutional requirement or in line with the general pattern of conformity. Social standardization thus means the thwarting of biological individual differences in function, and an acute problem for those who are trying to adjust their deviating personal characteristics to the system. Machine industry, which pushes the institutional mode up to the highest point in order to conform with a standardized pace of the machinery, is an extreme example. The worries and tensions which workers experience in their efforts to adjust their individual differences to this standard requirement play their part in the familiar occupational neuroses. In lesser degree, perhaps, the same problem arises throughout most of our business and professional life (3, p. 247).[1]

Not all observers of the industrial scene have agreed with the dire representations of industrial organization offered by social critics. Mary Parker Follett, the practical philosopher whose writings during the 1920s and 1930s had a significant impact on the thinking of many professors and some administrators, argued strenuously that organizations need not be frustrating or debasing to workers (109). In her view, the personal needs of members can be reconciled with the major purposes and requirements of organization, and all conflicts can be resolved "integratively"—in a way that is advantageous to everyone. But this hope requires attention to problems of "human relations" in a way that has been lacking in most approaches to administration. Many who share Follett's view see justification for her optimism in the results of the Hawthorne experiments. This research seemed to provide concrete evidence for the power of "human relations" in organizations and, more significantly, it offered some clues to how this power might be tapped.

[1] For a further, detailed analysis of the conflict between man and organization, see Argyris (9, 11) who argues that the work organization requires many members to act in immature rather than adult ways.

Thus, the Hawthorne research has become one of the corner-stones of the "human-relations movement" in industry. A chief pro-ponent of this movement was a Harvard Business School professor named Elton Mayo. Mayo stressed the overriding commonality of inter-est of all persons in the industrial organization. Conflict in organizations was for him a manifestation of "social disease"; cooperation was the more normal, "healthy" state of affairs. The Hawthorne test room epit-omized for Mayo the kind of spontaneous cooperation that is latent in every industrial organization. Furthermore, it had the qualities of Fol-lett's integrative solution: management's goal of efficiency advanced at the same time that the workers furthered their own "self-interest"; the girls earned higher wages, and what is more, they derived a considerable degree of satisfaction from their work.

This last point has not been lost on psychologists who have a natu-ral penchant for studying satisfaction and other indices of personal ad-justment. These variables in the organizational setting are distinctly psychological rather than administrative, sociological, or economic. Fur-thermore, these variables seemed to hold the key to productive efficiency —provided that the results of the Hawthorne experiments had any validity. For psychologists to have believed otherwise would have been less than natural.

Because some industrial managers also became interested in the possible relationship between job satisfaction and productivity, a grow-ing number of studies since the 1930s have investigated (a) the atti-tudes of workers toward their work and (b) the relationships of these at-titudes to productivity and to other factors on the job.

Morale and Worker Performance

Psychologists plunged into the study of morale and productivity with a mixture of faith and scientific zeal, setting out to document in business and industrial organizations generally what the Hawthorne research seemed to imply for the Western Electric test room: that the satisfied worker is a productive worker. Approximately thirty years and as many research studies later, however, psychologists must admit that the results of these studies are disappointingly tenuous. Some studies did show a positive association between the morale of workers and their level of productivity; but it is not always clear that positive attitudes *caused* the high productivity rather than vice versa. Moreover, the relationships found in many of these studies are weak, a number of the studies show no relationship at all, and a few even suggest a negative association.[2] In some cases, the results of these analyses were ironic. For example, Figure 4–1 shows the relationship between the productivity of a group of office workers and their participation in their company's recreational program. The figure shows that workers in high-producing sections participated less in the recreation program than did those in the low-producing sections. These recreational activities, which were designed at some expense to boost the morale of employees, obviously did not have the desired effect on the workers' productive efforts.

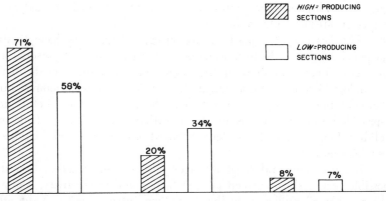

FIGURE 4–1. *Percentages of employees in high- and in low-producing work sections who participate in company recreational activities.* (Adapted from Katz et al., 81, p. 58.)

Psychologists do not agree fully about the meaning of these researches, but apparently the relationship between worker attitudes and productivity is not a direct and simple one. One weakness in the hypothesis that associates productivity with satisfaction is the failure to distinguish between satisfaction and motivation. Insofar as his needs are met, a person may be satisfied with his work. But his satisfaction indi-

[2] For comprehensive reviews and commentaries on such studies, see Brayfield and Crockett (30), Herzberg et al. (70), Katzell (83, pp. 243–244), and Likert (92, Chap. 2).

cates little about his motivation to work—particularly when his satisfaction does not depend on the amount of effort he puts into his work. Although job satisfaction may sometimes be associated with high productivity, as it evidently was in the Hawthorne test room, both of these variables are likely to be part of a more complex set of relationships.

Other indices of worker performance, however, may bear a more direct relationship to job satisfaction than does productivity. Measures of turnover and absenteeism, for example, correlate negatively with indices of worker morale (70, 169). Persons who dislike their jobs or their working conditions usually withdraw in one way or another. For example, Ross and Zander found significant differences between two kinds of female skilled workers in a large company (127): those who quit were less satisfied with the recognition they obtained on their jobs, with their sense of achievement, and with their degree of autonomy than were those who continued their employment. Mann and Baumgartel (103) compared work groups that had high absence rates with groups that had low absence rates, and found that workers in the latter groups were relatively more satisfied than the others with their jobs, supervisors, work associates, wages, promotional opportunities, and the company in general. Figure 4–2, taken from the Mann-Baumgartel study, shows the relationship between absenteeism and satisfaction with wages for white-collar men.

PER CENT SATISFIED WITH PRESENT WAGES

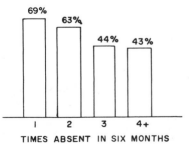

FIGURE 4–2. *Relationship between absenteeism and satisfaction with wages.* (From Mann and Baumgartel, 103, p. 19.)

Thus, although members' feelings of satisfaction are not directly related to productivity, these feelings do affect absenteeism and turnover. Furthermore, the satisfactions and dissatisfactions of members reflect important adjustments and conflicts in the organization. What are some of the factors that explain these adjustments and conflicts? We can begin our answer to this question by observing the effects of one of the most rudimentary elements of formal organization—the organizational hierarchy.

Hierarchy and Adjustment

The data of Figure 4–3 were collected during World War II by a group of psychologists, sociologists, and statisticians who produced the first major statistical study of attitudes in a large organization (150). This figure shows a relationship for the U.S. Army that is typical of the

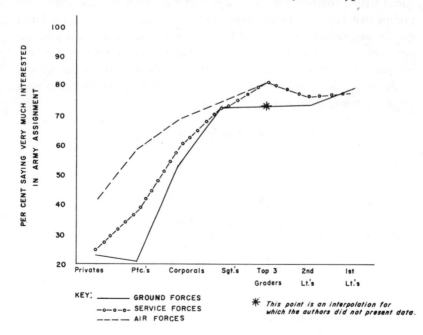

KEY: ——— GROUND FORCES
      –o–o–o– SERVICE FORCES
      – – – – AIR FORCES

✱ *This point is an interpolation for which the authors did not present data.*

FIGURE 4–3. *Interest in army job among officers and enlisted men.* (Adapted from Stouffer et al., 150, p. 307.)

work organization; that is, persons at higher ranks are generally more interested in or satisfied with their jobs than are persons at lower levels. They are also more involved and personally identified with their work, and their attitudes toward the organization itself are more favorable. These relationships are so general that students of organization may react with surprise when exceptions to them are found.

Organizational hierarchies are marked by several formal gradients, which correlate with job satisfaction as shown in Figure 4–3. These gradients are basic in explaining the relationship between rank and adjustment. Although we shall discuss them under three separate headings, the elements under each heading are interrelated.

Authority

Authority is generally distributed hierarchically in organizations. Individuals at upper levels have more power and exercise more control than those at successively lower levels. This distribution of power has an important impact on job satisfaction. Studies of organizations are reasonably consistent in showing a positive relationship between job satisfaction and the amount of control a person exercises in his work situation (26). Having some say in the affairs of the work situation contributes also to a member's sense of involvement in his work and in the organization, as well as his identification, personal commitment, and feeling of responsibility on the job.

The explanation for these relationships lies partly in the fact that organization members generally prefer exercising influence to being powerless—although there certainly are individual differences in this regard. Results from a number of studies show that workers and supervisors are more likely to feel that they have too little authority than too much. For example, several thousand workers in a large number of organizations were asked to describe how much control various groups in their workplace exercised and how much these groups *should* exercise. In 98 per cent of these organizations, the "average" worker felt that the workers as a whole did not have as much control as they should (154).

Managers—all the way to the pinnacle of the organization—feel that they, too, have too little power. Figure 4–4 shows differences between the amount of authority associated with managerial positions and the amount that persons in these positions feel they should have. Porter obtained these data in a survey of nearly two thousand managers employed in a variety of companies (121). He questioned each manager about the following authority-related aspects of his position:

1. The authority connected with the position.

2. The opportunity in it for independent thought and action.

3. The opportunity for participation in the setting of goals.

4. The opportunity for participation in the determination of methods and procedures.

Porter asked two questions relative to each of these dimensions:

a. How much is there now?
(min.)   1   2   3   4   5   6   7   (max.)

b. How much should there be?
(min.)   1   2   3   4   5   6   7   (max.)

For each dimension and each respondent, Porter subtracted the answer to question *a* from the answer to *b*. He refers to this difference as the *perceived deficiency in need fulfillment*. Positive scores imply that managers do not find as much authority in their positions as they want, and negative scores mean that they find more than they want. Since the perceived deficiencies in need fulfillment for each of the four authority-related aspects of the job follow essentially the same pattern, the results have been combined into the single index shown in Figure 4–4.

There are two important points to note in this figure. First, the average scores are *positive;* organization members generally perceive themselves as having less authority than they should have or would like to have. Second, the perceived discrepancies distinctly decrease with hierarchical ascent; persons at upper levels are likely to experience less dissatisfaction relative to their power or authority-related needs than are persons below them.

Status

Persons at higher levels are formally assigned greater status in the organization than persons at lower levels. Accordingly, persons at higher levels are considered more important and have greater responsibility, official respectability, and recognition. They also receive higher pay and enjoy greater privileges and perquisites: stock options, longer vaca-

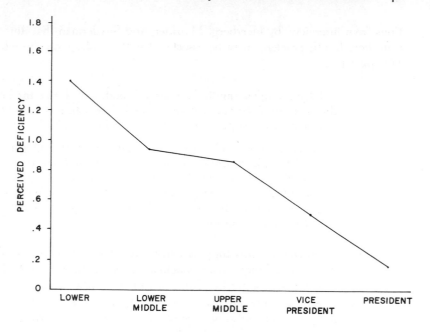

MANAGEMENT LEVELS

FIGURE 4–4. *Perceived deficiency in fulfillment of authority-related needs among managerial personnel.* (Adapted from Porter, 121. Professor Porter provided additional data upon which this figure is based.)

tions, and paid sick leaves. The responsibility, respect, and recognition, along with the greater material rewards associated with status, contribute significantly to the satisfaction of important needs—*and to a sense of self-esteem.*

Porter asked his managerial respondents how much self-esteem they get from their positions and how much they *should* get, and he again found a positive relationship between need fulfillment and hierarchical rank (121). Persons at higher levels feel less deprived than do those below them in their sense of self-esteem.

There are indications that status and self-esteem (which accompanies status) affect not only the satisfactions of organization members, but also their mental and physical health. Here are a couple of quota-

tions from interviews by Herzberg, Mausner, and Snyderman that illustrate how health problems may be associated with problems on the job
(69, pp. 91–92):

> I have angina [an inflammatory condition of the throat
> that may produce suffocative spasms]. Every time I have a
> run-in with my supervisor I get an attack.

> When I came back and found that my chief had gone
> over my head in dealing with my section without telling me,
> I realized I was on the skids here. I started drinking and
> smoking too much. Never had an auto accident before but
> I banged up my fenders twice during that month. I must
> have lost twenty pounds.

Because research on this topic is extremely difficult to perform, it
is not possible to draw unqualified conclusions. Nevertheless, some of
the available research data are helpful. For example, in a study of two
organizations Kasl and French made the assumption (based partly on
earlier research) that the seeking of medical aid and the reporting of
physical symptoms provides an index of mental ill health (77). These
authors found that the number of visits of employees to the company
dispensary, not including visits for injuries, correlates negatively with
self-esteem (which in turn is positively related to status).

Figure 4–5 illustrates the relationship Kasl and French found between job status and visits to the company dispensary for nonsupervisory
and for supervisory employees. Within each of these groups, the higher
the organization member's status (and self-esteem), the less likely he is
to visit the company dispensary. The high rate of dispensary visits at the
low-status supervisory level may be the result of an increase in responsibility at that point. This increase could be a source of worry or tension
leading to health problems for some supervisors. Aside from this apparent exception, however, the data generally show a negative relationship between status and what Kasl and French call "illness behavior."
Furthermore, these authors demonstrated that dispensary visits decreased
among a group of men who moved into higher-status jobs, whereas visits
increased for those who moved down in status.

Skill

As we move up the organization hierarchy, we find that jobs usually
require more skill. At higher levels, jobs are also less repetitious, rou-

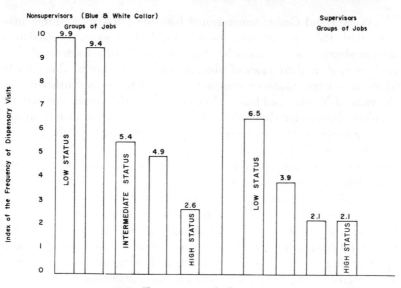

FIGURE 4–5. *Frequency of dispensary visits on supervisory and nonsupervisory jobs in a company.* (From Kasl and French, 77.)

tinized, and fractionated; and they allow greater discretion and choice to organization members. Accordingly, jobs at upper levels permit greater individuality to members and a greater sense of self-fulfillment or "self-actualization." At lower levels, however, a worker may experience serious frustrations because his job fails to provide sufficient opportunity for him to use his abilities or to realize his potential.

Among the jobs most frustrating to workers are the low-skill jobs on assembly lines. Walker and Guest made detailed studies of the problems encountered by workers on assembly lines in automobile plants and concluded that mass-production technology eliminates "virtually everything that might be of real, personal value to the worker" (59, p. 502). The words of one worker interviewed by Walker and Guest convey the frustration and despair of many employees on the assembly line:

> You can't beat the machine. They have you clocked to a fraction of a second. My job is engineered, and the jigs and fixtures are all set out according to specifications. The foreman is an all right guy, but he gets pushed, so he pushes us. The guy on the line has no one to push. You can't fight that iron horse (171, p. 71).

Walker and Guest demonstrated how the low-skill requirements—along with the repetitiveness, routine, and lack of social interaction of mass-production jobs—adversely affect workers' attitudes toward their work as well as their rates of absenteeism and tardiness. Research by Morse in a large insurance company (112, Chap. 4) is consistent with the work of Walker and Guest. In clerical jobs, the greater the skill demanded, the greater the variety offered, and the more discretion and choice allowed to clerks in their work operations, the greater the job satisfaction the workers were likely to experience. Moreover, the increased satisfaction is not simply the result of the higher pay that often compensates skill. Morse demonstrated that the positive relationship between use of skill and job satisfaction exists regardless of pay level.

Some of the effects of low-skill jobs might be gleaned more readily from an analysis of workers who adjust well to such jobs than from those who have difficulty adjusting. Argyris considered this possibility by broaching a subject about which relatively little information is available because of its "touchiness"—the success of mentally retarded workers (11, pp. 66–67). Argyris quotes Brennan's description of two instances in which mentally retarded persons were successfully employed on unskilled jobs in a knitting mill and in a radio-manufacturing corporation. In both cases, the managers praised these employees for their excellence. In the knitting mill, the retarded girls "were more punctual, more regular in their habits, and did not indulge in as much 'gossip and levity.' " In the radio corporation,

> the girls proved to be exceptionally well-behaved, particularly obedient, and strictly honest and trustworthy. They carried out work required of them to such a degree of efficiency that *we were surprised they were classed as subnormals for their age*. Their attendance was good, and their behavior was, if anything, certainly better than that of any other employee of the same age (31, pp. 13–18, as quoted in 11; italics in original).

These dramatic illustrations do not mean that all low-skill jobs are designed for morons (although some jobs may be appropriate to this level of intelligence). Several studies suggest that within normal ranges, I.Q. alone does not affect workers' job satisfaction (70, 144, 169, pp. 135–138). *Education*, however, does sometimes lead to dissatisfaction (102, 112). An unpublished analysis by Mann shows that the negative correlation between education and job satisfaction is most striking for workers on unskilled jobs, is less strong for semiskilled workers, and is entirely absent for employees doing skilled work.

The education level of the work force has risen over the years, and it will continue to rise. With education, workers acquire abilities as well as aspirations which may not be easily realized. Thus, unskilled jobs at the lower levels of the hierarchy do not always match the capacities and aspirations of members. In mass-production operations particularly, jobs impose physical as well as mental constraints on workers. Such jobs cannot stimulate, challenge, or interest workers, and workers are therefore likely to perform them with less than a sense of complete involvement.

Hierarchy and Conflict

Hierarchy is a basic *organizational* characteristic, but it has the most profound *psychological* implications for the individual members. In the hierarchy, persons work together but are rewarded and motivated differently. Persons at higher levels are not only paid more; they are awarded greater *psychological* compensation. Organization, therefore is more or less compatible with the self-interests of members, depending partly on where they are in the organization hierarchy.

Organization, then, implies a kind of class society in the sense that, psychologically and economically, some members are more advantageously situated in it than others. Some members may also *give* more to the organization in the intensities of their involvements and efforts. It is not surprising therefore to find serious conflicts between persons in different positions. Symptoms of conflict, or of the potential for conflict, can be seen in three general differences between echelons in addition to the satisfaction gradients discussed above: (1) differences in perceptions and cognitions; (2) differences in ideals and norms; and (3) differences in loyalty.

Differences in Perceptions and Cognitions

Persons in different hierarchical positions may perceive or interpret important events in the organization quite differently. These differences are to be understood partly in terms of the principle mentioned in Chapter 3: perceptions and cognitions are affected by motivational states. Persons in different positions are motivated in different ways. They also have different sources of information and vantage points from which to view organizational events. Moreover, their immediate social and psychological environments are strikingly and systematically different. For example, the president interacts frequently with his vice-presidents and others at the executive level, whereas employees interact primarily with their co-workers and supervisors. These diverse groups live in worlds that are radically different. Furthermore, their worlds are composed in a number of respects, of *like-minded* individuals. Since persons at higher levels are more satisfied with and interested in their work than are those at lower levels, the president is in frequent touch with persons who share his relatively rosy picture of organizational life. These highly involved and interested persons feel relatively little dissatisfaction regarding authority, self-esteem, and self-actualization. It should not be surprising therefore to find them wondering occasionally why *everyone* in the organization does not have the same enthusiastic view they have. On the other hand, persons at the bottom of the hierarchy live in a psychologically depressed area, and each of them has considerable support from his fellow workers for his relatively jaundiced view of organizational life.

A number of research studies have documented some of the different perceptions and cognitions that are a function of hierarchical position. For example, Morse asked a group of clerical workers and their supervisors, "How does a person get ahead here in the company?" She found that supervisors were more likely than workers to explain advancement in terms of "merit," whereas workers were more likely to explain it more cynically (if not more realistically), in terms of "knowing the right people, or luck" (112, p. 100).

Striking perceptual differences also occur between persons at managerial levels. Maier, Hoffman, Hooven, and Read asked high-level managers and their immediate managerial subordinates to describe aspects of the subordinates' jobs. Table 4–1 shows the amount of agreement and disagreement within these managerial superior-subordinate pairs. Even though written job descriptions were available, only about 46 per cent of the pairs agreed on more than half of the topics concerning the job duties of the subordinates. A considerably greater discrepancy in perception can be noted with regard to the obstacles which these persons see as preventing the subordinate from performing well on the job. Needless to say, potential (if not real) conflict exists when a supervisor and his subordinate characteristically see different kinds of things interfering with the subordinate's doing his job.

TABLE 4–1. *Comparative agreement between superior-subordinate pairs on basic areas of the subordinate's job.* (Percentages based on study of 58 pairs. Adapted from 99, p. 10.)

	Agreement on less than half the topics	Agreement on about half the topics	Agreement on more than half the topics
Job duties	15.0%	39.1%	45.9%
Obstacles in the way of subordinate's performance	68.2%	23.6%	8.1%

Part of the difficulty arises from authority and status differences, which inhibit members from communicating freely with their superiors about important job matters. Thus, the different perceptions between subordinates and supervisors are likely to remain differences. This problem of communication is illustrated in Table 4–2, based on a study by

TABLE 4–2. *Extent to which superiors and subordinates agree on aspects of communication between them.* (From 102.)

	% Top staff say about foremen	% Foremen say about themselves	% Foremen say about the men	% Men say about themselves
Feel very free to discuss important things about the job with superior	90	67	85	51
Always or nearly always tell subordinates in advance about changes which will affect them or their work	100	63	92	47
Always or almost always get subordinates' ideas	70	52	73	16

Mann in a large public utility. The table presents results of several parallel questions asked of workers, their foremen, and top staff. The first row indicates that between 85 and 90 per cent of the foremen and of top staff think that their subordinates feel very free to discuss important job matters with them. However, only about half of the men and two-thirds of the foremen say that they feel very free to discuss important matters with their superiors. The second and third rows tell a similar story. Superiors are more likely than subordinates to think that communications between them are good.

Research has also revealed significant discrepancies in the perceptions by one hierarchical group of the motives or attitudes of another. Motives and attitudes are ambiguous referents, of course, and differences are to be expected. Yet the character of these differences is significant. For example, in their classic study of adjustment to army life, Stouffer and his colleagues found that officers overestimate enlisted men's (a) desire to be soldiers, (b) satisfaction with their jobs, (c) importance which they attach to the infantry, and (d) pride in their companies. To the question "How many of your officers are the kind who are willing to go through anything they ask their men to go through?" 92 per cent of the officers, but only 37 per cent of the enlisted men, answered "all" or "most." When asked to react to the statement "Most enlisted men do *not* respect their officers," only 25 per cent of officers, compared to 54 per cent of the enlisted men, agreed (150, p. 395). One reason for the officers' misjudging this basic fact of organizational life is that many men *act* as if they respect their officers when in fact they do not respect their officers.

Table 4–3, based on a study by R. L. Kahn in a large appliance-manufacturing company (75), shows the results of two questions asked of members at different ranks. Workers were asked only the first question; supervisory and managerial persons were asked both:

1. Different people want different things out of a job. What are the things you yourself feel are *most important* in a job?

2. Different people want different things out of a job. What are the things you think most of the people you supervise feel are *most important* in a job?

All of the respondents were shown the list of variables in Table 4–3. Kahn stresses several highlights of this table:

1. Foremen and general foremen misjudge the importance their subordinates attach to some, if not all, qualities of the subordinates' jobs.

TABLE 4–3. *What subordinates want in a job, compared with their superiors' estimates.* (From Kahn, 75. Reprinted by permission of author and publisher.)

	AS MEN	AS FOREMEN		AS GENERAL FOREMEN	
	Rated the variables for themselves	Estimated men would rate the variables	Rated the variables for themselves	Estimated foremen would rate the variables	Rated the variables for themselves
Economic variables:					
Steady work and steady wages	61%	79%	62%	86%	52%
High wages	28	61	17	58	11
Pensions and other old-age-security benefits	13	17	12	29	15
Not having to work too hard	13	30	4	25	2
Human-satisfaction variables:					
Getting along well with the people I work with	36%	17%	39%	22%	43%
Getting along well with my supervisor	28	14	28	15	24
Good chance to turn out good-quality work	16	11	18	13	27
Good chance to do interesting work	22	12	38	14	43
Other variables:					
Good chance for promotion	25%	23%	42%	24%	47%
Good physical working conditions	21	19	18	4	11
Total	*	*	*	*	*
Number of cases	2,499	196	196	45	45

* Percentages total over 100 because they include three rankings for each person.

2. Supervisors overestimate the desire of workers for economic rewards and for "not having to work too hard."

3. Supervisors underestimate the importance that subordinates attach to "social approval and self-expression—getting on well with one's supervisor and fellow workers, and having a chance to do work of high quality and interesting content" (75, p. 50).

4. These discrepancies in perception apply also to general foremen's ratings of foremen as well as to foremen's ratings of workers.

5. Supervisors apparently misperceive the job attitudes of their subordinates despite some basic similarities in what both groups want from their jobs. For example, 28 per cent of the men and 28 per cent of the foremen personally attach great importance to "getting along well with my supervisor"; yet only 14 per cent of foremen and 15 per cent of the general foremen ascribe this attitude to their subordinates—which indicates that the superior may be more like his subordinate than he thinks he is.

Differences in Ideals and Norms for the Organization

Persons express different ideals for their organization. In crucial respects, the kind of organization that workers want is a different kind from that preferred by their supervisors and managers. On the question of authority, for example, a compilation of results from a number of studies of work organizations reveals that workers, on the average, want to exercise more control over what goes on in the workplace than they perceive themselves to exercise. However, in none of these organizations do *supervisors* want workers as a group to exercise more control than they are perceived to be exercising. Simply put, employees are likely to want a more democratic organization than supervisors want. By way of contrast, research in a *voluntary* organization, the League of Women Voters, showed that officers are as likely as members to prefer a democratic distribution of control (143).

The study of the American soldier to which we have referred provides further documentation for the important attitudinal and ideological differences that exist between ranks. Army discipline, which implies emphasis on "spit and polish" and "military courtesy," was generally regarded as desirable by most officers but as undesirable by enlisted men (150). Table 4–4 illustrates in more concrete detail how rank makes a difference in the preference which enlisted men, noncommissioned officers, and officers express regarding some of the standards of comportment for noncommissioned officers. Admittedly, most of these differences are not surprising; but they are nonetheless significant in reflecting the underlying bases of conflict within the organization. In small ways and in large, rank-and-file members tell us they want one kind of organization, and officers tell us they want another.

TABLE 4–4. *Comparisons of privates, noncoms, and officers on attitudes toward noncom behavior.* (From 150, p. 408.)

	PER CENT WHO AGREE WITH EACH STATEMENT		
	PRIVATES (384)	NONCOMS (195)	OFFICERS (31)
SOCIAL RELATIONS			
"A noncom will lose some of the respect of his men if he pals around with them off-duty"	13	16	39
"A noncom should not let the men in his squad forget that he is a noncom even when off-duty"	39	54	81
DISCIPLINE			
"A noncom has to be very strict with his men or else they will take advantage of him"	45	52	68
"A noncom should teach his men to obey all rules and regulations without questioning them"	63	81	90
WORK SUPERVISION			
"A noncom should always keep his men busy during duty hours, even if he has to make them do unnecessary work"	16	22	39
"The harder a noncom works his men the more respect they will have for him"	10	18	42
"On a fatigue detail, a noncom should see that the men under him get the work done, but should not help them do it"	36	37	68

Numbers in parentheses are the numbers of cases.

In the work organization, the preferences of officers correspond more closely than those of rank-and-file members to the official ideals of the organization. The operation of the organization, however, may conform more closely to what rank-and-file members want than to the wishes of officers. For example, a study of productivity and attitudes of workers and their foremen showed that (a) the level of productivity considered reasonable by workers is below that considered reasonable by their foremen, (b) the level considered reasonable by foremen is below that officially considered reasonable by the company, (c) most workers are producing at levels considerably below the official norm and below the level considered reasonable by their supervisors, and (d) the actual level of production corresponds more closely to what workers consider reasonable than to what their foremen or higher company officials consider reasonable (92, p. 48).

Differences in Loyalty and Support for the Organization

Superiors are more likely than their subordinates to identify with the organization and to support it psychologically; organizational policies and actions are more likely to seem to them morally correct, fair, and just. Superiors are more likely to take the view that what is good for the organization is good for *all* its members. The study of productivity that we have just reported, for example, showed that foremen are closer to accepting as reasonable the company policy regarding productivity than are the men. The foremen's immediate superiors in turn can be expected to agree more with the official productivity standard than do the foremen—and so on up the organizational hierarchy.

A member's attitudes of support for the organization and its policies are likely to change as his position in the hierarchy changes. Workers who become foremen, for example, are likely to adopt attitudes similar to the attitudes of other foremen, and different from the attitudes of workers. This process of increasing loyalty and support that accompanies increasing rank has been investigated by Lieberman (90). This psychologist administered attitude questionnaires to more than two thousand workers in a large appliance-manufacturing concern. A year later, twenty-three workers who had been promoted to the rank of foreman and a group of workers who had not been promoted completed the questionnaire again. Workers in both groups were matched on a number of demographic characteristics, such as age and education, and on their responses to the initial questionnaire. Although both groups showed essentially the same attitudes toward the company and its policies on the first questionnaire, the data from the second questionnaire indicated that the foremen had changed to greater agreement with and support for the organization and its policies. The foremen felt that the company was concerned about the welfare of workers; they saw the union as an impediment to the organization; they changed markedly in their support for the controversial company incentive system; and they showed some shift in the direction of adopting the company's point of view rather than the union's on the issue of seniority as the basis for promotion.

Some time after Lieberman had given the second questionnaire, the nation suffered an economic recession. As a result, the company returned eight of the foremen to worker status. Twelve others remained foremen and three left the company for unrelated reasons. Lieberman administered his questionnaire again and found that the demoted foremen had regained their original attitudes. Not only do persons change toward agreement with company policy as they move up the hierarchy, but they change away from agreement as they move down.

Lieberman also compared the attitudes of workers who were elected union stewards with the attitudes of workers who were promoted to foremen. Figure 4–6 indicates the changes these two groups underwent. It is based on the responses of twelve foremen and six union stewards

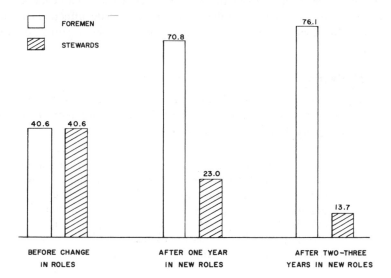

FIGURE 4–6. *Effects of foreman and steward roles: Per cent who express pro-management attitudes.* (Adapted from 90, p. 398.)

who remained in their new roles about three years. The percentages in the figure represent the average proportions of the foremen and stewards who took a distinctly pro-management position on sixteen attitude measures.

Before their selection, these foremen and stewards did not differ in their attitudes toward the company and its policies. One year after assuming their new positions, however, the two groups diverged sharply, and after several years, they moved even further apart. On the basis of the data in this figure and other analyses, Lieberman concluded that differences in attitude between company foremen and union stewards do *not* result from the selection of pro-company workers as foremen nor the election of anti-company workers as stewards. Apparently, foremen and stewards acquire their attitudes as they move up their respective hierarchies.

Adjustment, Conflict, and Organizational Performance

The problems of adjustment and conflict which we have discussed affect organizational performance in a number of ways: (a) they reduce the motivation of many members, (b) they impede effective control and coordination, and (c) they create opposition to the organization and its leaders.

Motivation

The success of the organization depends on the member's willingness to work assiduously and constructively in helping achieve the organization's goals. This willingness requires that

> each member of the organization . . . feel that the organization's objectives are of significance and that his own particular task contributes in an indispensable manner to the organization's achievement of its objectives. He should see his role as difficult, important, and meaningful. This is necessary if the individual is to achieve and maintain a sense of personal worth and importance (92, p. 103).

As we have seen through the data cited in this chapter, organizations do not fully meet this requirement—especially insofar as rank-and-file members are concerned.

Peter Blau, a sociological theorist, sees the motivational problem of organizational hierarchy this way:

> In a democracy . . . where status prerogatives are frowned upon, intense feelings of inequality among the lower echelons of a bureaucracy have several effects that are detrimental for operations. They inhibit identification with the organization and its objectives, lessen interest in performing tasks to the best of one's abilities, kill initiative, and reduce the chances that emergent operating problems will be readily met. Unless employees consider themselves partners in a common enterprise rather than tools in the hands of management, they are not prone willingly to assume responsibilities of their own (25, p. 80).

Control

Control and coordination are essential to any organized effort. A supervisor, however, can not exercise effective control over subordinates when his information about them is in serious error, and when he and they base their actions on seriously differing perceptions. At the very least, discrepancies in members' perceptions and cognitions make the job of control and coordination more difficult; at worst, they contribute—in the context of differences in rewards, satisfactions, interests, ideals, involvements, and loyalties—to resentment, distrust, hostility, and opposition.

Opposition

Opposition to the organization and its leaders, can manifest itself in various ways. It may express itself as a mild form of "passive resistance." Subordinates may simply withhold important information from their supervisors, keeping them in the dark about matters concerning which they should be informed. In some instances, subordinates may develop useful ideas for improving the product, or the work process, or the organization itself, but will not pass these on. Workers on jobs designed by time-study engineers, for example, may invent (often with considerable ingenuity) an "arsenal of secret weapons" such as jigs and fixtures that help them do their jobs more efficiently than is possible with the official method (176, p. 17). These workers do not always reveal their inventions to management, however, because they assume, sometimes realistically, that management will reset job rates. Such employees often hold these inventions in reserve to ease their jobs when the supervisor is not looking.

Certain forms of absenteeism, tardiness, "goldbricking," and slowdowns may also represent opposition that is relatively passive but nonetheless sometimes costly. Opposition may manifest itself in more aggressive forms too. Disputes, grievances, and strikes are the more aggressive forms of opposition, which workers employ through their unions. Employees may even resort to sabotage, although this is rare.

Forms of opposition of the type just described are symptoms of the "social disease," which Elton Mayo argues need not exist—except in organizations that do not conform to sophisticated principles of human relations. Organizations, in fact, differ in the degree to which they are subject to opposition, and one of our purposes is to understand why some organizations are relatively free of opposition while others verge on collapse because of it. The Hawthorne research offered a clue in answer to this question by revealing that opposition and cooperation frequently occur not as reactions of individual members but as collective reactions of members through groups. We shall consider these group reactions in the next chapter.

chapter five

The Group
in Organizations

The Hawthorne studies were a revelation to students of organization in dramatizing the importance of social groups in industry. At the same time, and quite independently of the Hawthorne research, social psychologists were experimenting with groups in college laboratories. This research elucidated two processes that have important effects in the work organization. The first is *conformity;* groups develop norms or standards of comportment to which members conform. The second is *support;* groups provide comfort or aid to their members, particularly in frustrating or threatening environments.

We shall examine in this chapter how these group processes affect the adjustments and performance of organization members. It will be useful to start by reviewing briefly some of what has been learned about these processes through laboratory research.

Conformity

In the 1920s F. H. Allport reported the results of several experiments he conducted among graduate students at Harvard (4). In these experiments the students made judgments about the weights of objects and the pleasantness or unpleasantness of odors. The students made these judgments alone and in the presence of others, and each subject recorded his judgments on paper without revealing them to the other subjects. Allport found that subjects made less extreme evaluations in the presence of others than when alone. Although the subjects did not know the judgments of others in the group, they imagined how the others were reacting and they avoided what they thought would be extreme and deviant responses. Allport attributed this moderation of judgment to an "attitude of social conformity" that persons adopt in social situations, even in the absence of communication among them.

Normally, members of a group communicate with one another, and Sherif demonstrated how members develop common standards as they become aware of the opinions of others in the group (140). He placed subjects in a darkened room where they could observe a pinpoint of light. Although the light does not move, most persons experience the illusion of movement, an illusion known as the *autokinetic effect*. Subjects who experience this effect while alone establish individual norms representing the average distances which they judge the light to move. However, subjects tested in groups gradually alter their individual judgments to agree more closely with the judgments reported by the others in their group. A common standard thus becomes established as the norm for the group.

Once a norm is established, members do not deviate easily from it, and some members may conform even against their "better" judgment. Asch asked persons in groups to estimate which of three lines of varying lengths was equal to a fourth line (12). Only one person in each experimental group, however, was a real subject; the others pretended to be subjects but were really confederates of the experimenter, instructed to make erroneous judgments. The lone subject was therefore confronted with others who, in direct contradiction to the subject's own senses, unanimously and repeatedly chose the wrong line. About one third of the real subjects who underwent this experience changed their reported judgments to conform to that of the group—even though the lengths of the lines were not the least bit ambiguous, as demonstrated by subjects who made virtually no errors in judgment when not confronted with contrary group pressures.

These studies illustrate the power of the group as an instrument of influence or control over members. However, not all groups are equally effective in establishing or maintaining conformity. Festinger, Schachter, Back, and others have investigated group conditions that are conducive to conformity (16, 47, 48, 130). These psychologists find support in their research for a number of propositions, of which we list three:

1. The more attractive a group is to members, the more likely members are to change their views to conform with those of others in the group.

2. If an individual fails to conform, the group is likely to reject him; and the more attractive the group is to its members, the more decisively they will reject this individual.

3. Members are more likely to be rejected for deviancy on an issue that is important to the group than on an issue that is unimportant.

These propositions suggest that members, implicitly or explicitly, demand conformity because it helps maintain the group that is "attractive" to them. A general basis for the attractiveness of the group is the satisfaction that people derive from their social relations in it. In the work organization informal social behaviors—friendly remarks, jokes, and conversations about matters of mutual interest—give expression to many personal needs that are frustrated by the formal limits of work roles. Groups also provide *support* to their members, and this is an especially important basis for members' attraction to the group in the context of the frustration members face on the job.

Support

Support by a group occurs in several forms. When members face a frustrating or threatening environment, the group may (a) afford some sense of comfort or consolation to members, (b) help or protect members by acting against the source of threat or frustration, and (c) strengthen the individual member in his own opposition to the source of adversity.

Research by Schachter illustrates the comfort that persons undergoing threat derive through associating with others in a group (130). This psychologist compared the behavior of two groups of college students. Subjects in the first group were told they would undergo an experiment involving severe electric shock, while those in the second group were instructed that the experiment would involve only a very slight shock, equivalent to a tickle. The experimenter then informed the subjects that they might choose to wait their turns alone or together with others. They were also told that in the "together" situation they would not be permitted to talk to one another. Schachter thus ruled out the possibility that the subjects who waited together might plan some joint action. Nonetheless nearly two thirds of the subjects in the "severe-shock" group preferred to wait in a room with others, whereas approximately the same proportion of subjects in the second group did not care whether they waited with others or alone.

Schachter's research suggests that people are drawn to each other *psychologically* under conditions of threat or frustration. We stress the word *psychologically* because there may be no apparent benefit to members from their affiliation beyond whatever gratification or comfort is derived from the mere presence of others. The group, in other words, need not *do* anything about the source of threat in order to attract members. However, groups can sometimes act or attempt to act against the source of threat, and they may in this way afford protection or hope of protection to members. Thus a pragmatic form of support may be added to the "psychological" support that comes from the mere presence of others. In Mulder and Stemerding's experiment with Dutch shopkeepers, both these forms of support appear (114). The shopkeepers were brought together in groups, and half of them were told that highly competitive supermarkets were about to open in their town. These threatened subjects—more than the remaining subjects, who were not threatened— wanted to continue in groups. The threatened subjects were attracted to a group partly because they hoped that the group might plan an effective campaign against the supermarkets and partly because they sought "psychological comfort" simply from associating with people who faced the same problem.

A group may also provide support to a member by strengthening him psychologically in his opposition to a source of frustration. Stotland, for example, found that subjects' reactions to a restrictive authority figure. during the course of an experiment were affected by their opportunities to talk to other subjects (148). Unlike those who had no social contact, subjects who spent some time with other subjects (a) were more aggressive and hostile toward their supervisor, (b) disagreed with the supervisor more often, (c) expressed greater dissatisfaction with the supervisor's failure to give reasons for his behavior, and (d) argued strenuously for *their own* positions as opposed to that of the supervisor.

Implications of the Group for the Work Organization

Organizations are full of informal face-to-face groups that offer satisfying interpersonal relations and support to their members in the face of frustrations on the job. These groups form among workers operating around a common machine, or among workers who are near one another on the shop floor, or among workers who meet at lunch or in rest rooms or while moving around the plant. Many such groups develop norms that are relevant to the performance of the job. Members who do not conform to the group's norms face disapproval, ostracism, or expulsion from the group. And if these sanctions fail, physical force may be employed. Thus relationships within these informal groups— particularly groups that are highly attractive to members—imply control and conformity as well as satisfactions and support. These characteristics help make group action the *concerted* or *mobilized* effort that it sometimes is.

Although these groups are informal—they are not in the official organization chart, nor are they part of the official chain of command— they can operate with considerable effectiveness as law-enforcement agencies within the larger, formal structure of the organization. Whether they oppose or support high levels of performance can mean the difference between success or failure for the organization. So let us take a closer look at how these groups operate in the work organization.

Effects of the Group on Adjustment

Near the end of World War II, mass-production technology was introduced into British coal mines, in order to make mining more efficient. However, the new methods produced some unexpected results (163). For instance, psychosomatic ailments of epidemic proportions broke out among miners, and worker morale dropped to a low ebb. Absenteeism, conflicts, and tensions among workers rapidly increased —and productivity did not rise as it should have. At fault was the new technology, which—however sound from an engineering standpoint— did not take into account some of the social and psychological facts of life for the miner on the job; it did not consider the function of the social group.

Coal mines are dark, lonely, and dangerous. The miners had coped with these adverse working conditions by forming small, tight-knit work groups. The members of these groups chose one another, knew one another, and relied on one another. Thus, they gained some sense of security against the dark, the danger, and other hardships of mining. Outside the mine, these supportive groups operated through the friendship and kinship relations within the community. When a miner died as a result of a mine accident, the members of his group often assumed responsibility for his family.

These group relations changed radically under the new technology. The new method of extracting coal relocated workers over a large area in the mine, so that they could no longer talk with one another easily. Their jobs, redefined by the new, large-scale machinery, isolated them further; they no longer collaborated closely and directly in getting the coal from the seam and out of the mine. Because of the new machinery, each worker specialized in a very limited part of the total process of extracting coal, which formerly was the responsibility of the group. Thus, the groups of mutually interdependent miners, which were functionally compatible with the earlier system of mining, became inappropriate. The mass-production technology disrupted these important social ties, and, where adjustments were not made to substitute new social arrangements for the old, the mental health, morale, and productive efforts of the miners suffered.

The soldier on the battlefield, like the worker in the mine, faces serious hazards, and research in the Army during World War II demonstrated the importance of groups under conditions of stress. The soldier replacement, for example, was a special problem because he might be sent into battle as part of a veteran unit before he had established social relations and friendships. "Being a replacement," as one soldier put it, "is just like being an orphan. You are away from anybody you know and feel lost and lonesome" (149, p. 273). Significantly, the most serious combat error that such replacements made on the battlefield was "bunching up" (huddling together in groups when under fire). M. Brewster Smith, who wrote the report on replacements, explains the problem this way:

> Bunching up under fire—gathering together for mutual psychological support—is a strong indication of feelings of insecurity. New replacements engaged in this practice in spite of its obvious dangers, and in spite of the emphasis in training doctrine upon dispersal under fire. The obvious irrationality of the action suggests the imperativeness of the motivation behind it (149, p. 284).

Bunching up was the most frequently reported error on the battlefield among combat veterans too. But seasoned troops committed this error less frequently than replacements.

Desertion among combat infantrymen is also partly a problem of soldiers' group relations. For example, Rose (125) found that AWOL's (soldiers away without leave) were less familiar with others in their outfits than were non-AWOL's. Forty-one per cent of the AWOL's he studied said they knew only a few or none of the other men well, while less than a third as many non-AWOL's suffered this degree of social isolation. Moreover, 80 per cent of the non-AWOL's said that they liked working with most of the men in their outfit, while only 62 per cent of the AWOL's felt this way. Rose emphasized the significance of these facts since earlier analyses showed that "pride in outfit" and desire "not to let the other fellows down" are central to the morale of combat soldiers (149).

Research on absenteeism and turnover in industry also suggest the importance of the group. Trist and Bamforth's study of British miners, reported above, illustrates some of the possible effects of groups on morale and on absenteeism. Research in other organizations generally supports the hypothesis that membership in a cohesive group helps increase job satisfaction and reduce absenteeism and turnover. Coch and French, for example, studied a group of textile workers who were required to adapt to changes in work methods. The turnover rates for these workers were quite high, but those who belonged to groups with strong "we feeling" quit at a much lower rate—even though they had strong antagonistic feelings toward the company—than those who did not belong to "cohesive" groups (36). Mann and Baumgartel show how a sense of group belongingness, group spirit, group pride, or group solidarity on the part of workers relates inversely to rates of absenteeism. Figure 5–1 illustrates one of these relationships for white-collar workers. In groups where workers were absent at least four times during a six-month period, only 21 per cent report that their crew is better than others in sticking together. However, 62 per cent of workers in groups with an average of only one absence during the six month period report this kind of cohesiveness among members.

Seashore investigated the effects of the cohesiveness of work groups on the adjustments of members among 228 work groups in a large, heavy-machinery-manufacturing company. He considers a group highly cohesive if the members "(1) perceive themselves to be a part of a group, (2) prefer to remain in the group rather than to leave, and (3) perceive their group to be better than other groups with respect to the way the men get along together, the way they help each other out, and the way

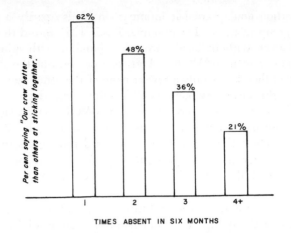

FIGURE 5–1. *Relationship between group solidarity and absenteeism among white-collar men.* (From 103, p. 14.)

they stick together" (132, p. 36). Seashore found that members of groups high in cohesiveness generally experienced fewer work-related anxieties than those in less cohesive groups. Figure 5–2 shows the relationship between group cohesiveness and the responses of members to the question: "Does your work ever make you feel 'jumpy' or nervous?" The more cohesive the group, the less likely its members are to feel "nervous" and "jumpy."

The group, then, appears to have important effects on the adjustment of organization members. In a number of respects, workers who belong to cohesive groups appear "better adjusted" in the organization than those who do not have these informal attachments. Workers who belong to such groups are likely to have higher rates of job satisfaction and lower rates of tension, absenteeism, and turnover than workers who do not belong to cohesive groups. The better adjustment of members of cohesive groups is due in part to the satisfactions and the psychological support that groups provide. The better adjustment may also reflect the lesser tendency for persons who are inept in social relations to join groups in the first place. But what implications does the group have for workers' productive efforts? Let us return to the Hawthorne study in our search for an answer to this question.

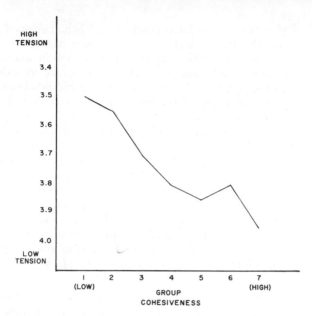

FIGURE 5–2. *Relationship between group co-hesiveness and tension at work.* (From 132, p. 49.)

Effects of the Group on Productivity

In the Hawthorne research, the formation of a tight-knit group in the relay-assembly test room seemed to be responsible for the steadily increasing productivity. Increased productivity, however, is not the inevitable result of cohesive groups. Quite the contrary: When cohesive groups are formed in opposition to the organization, productivity drops. Subsequent phases of the Hawthorne research made this point eminently clear.

The existence of opposition groups throughout the Hawthorne plant became evident when the researchers engaged in an interviewing program, following the relay-assembly test-room experiments:

> It was while the investigators were working in this way that their attention was first called to problems of employee interrelations and group organization. Their reports showed very clearly that they were encountering several related

phenomena, the importance of which had escaped them before this time. Chief among these was restriction of output. Although restriction in some form is not an uncommon occurrence and most industrialists recognize its existence in varying degrees, the investigators had hitherto been unaware of its implications for management practice and employee satisfaction. Some of the evidence obtained suggested that the wage-incentive systems under which some of the groups worked had been rendered ineffectual by group pressures for controlled output. Informal practices by means of which certain operators were placed under pressure and kept in line were brought to light. There was evidence of informal leadership on the part of certain persons who took upon themselves the responsibility of seeing that the members of a group clung together and protected themselves from representatives of other groups within the company who could interfere with their affairs (124, pp. 379–380).

As a result of this insight, the Hawthorne researchers set up a new test room, in order to observe in detail the social relations among a group of workers. Fourteen operators who assembled terminal banks for use in telephone exchanges were placed in a room called the *bank-wiring observation room*. This room was run quite differently from the relay test room. Insofar as possible, the social and psychological atmosphere was kept precisely what it was in the regular departments: supervision, work methods, privileges, methods of pay, and the rules and regulations governing workers' behavior were just what they were on the shop floor. Although an observer was present, his role was devoid of authority; the men were accountable to their regular supervisor. The observer's purpose was to gain the confidence of the men so that he could observe in detail their normal work behavior. (He was highly successful—as the results of his observations showed: after losing their initial constraint, the wiremen demonstrated their very effective techniques of restricting production and of fooling their supervisor.)

The men in the test room established norms to which they all conformed. One of these norms concerned the way they acted when the supervisor was present and when he was away: all was seriousness and industry in his presence; but in his absence, levity and relaxation were the rule. Furthermore, the wiremen established their own standard for production, and each employee consistently produced about what the group considered the "proper" amount of work.

It was apparent to the observer that the men maintained a lower level of production than they could very easily have achieved. They did this despite the "logic" of a wage-incentive system that would have rewarded them with larger pay checks, had they been less restrictive. In the *workers'* "logic," higher production would only lead the company to raise the piece rates, canceling out whatever additional earnings they might have made. The group, its restrictive norm, and its control over members were natural consequences of this state of conflict. This control applied to members who produced at levels below the informal norm as well as to those who exceeded it. Low producers were called "chiselers" and were admonished for not carrying their own weight. More often, however, the group imposed its sanctions on the "rate busters" or "slaves," who were producing at dangerously high levels.

Hawthorne drew the attention of social scientists to the group in industry, and soon a number of other researchers conducted studies on the effects of the group on worker productivity. Coch and French found that workers in informal social groups lowered their productivity in order to resist innovations in work methods introduced by the company, and that more cohesive groups—those with strong "we feeling"—provided greater support to members who opposed the innovations (36). Seashore showed that workers in cohesive groups were neither more nor less productive on the average than workers in noncohesive groups, but in the cohesive groups workers were more *uniform* in their productivity—they all produced pretty much the same amount (132).

This uniformity is brought about through pressures against deviancy. Figure 5–3 illustrates the effects of these pressures in changing the behavior of a newcomer to a group (36). A female textile worker, the newcomer unwittingly learned her job too well; and she began, after only a few days on the job, to exceed the group's production norm of about 50 units. On the thirteenth day, the group began to express its antagonism, with the desired effect: her productivity dropped. On the twentieth day, however, when all the members except the newcomer were transferred to other jobs, the group disbanded. Without the group to guide her productive efforts, her production climbed to an almost impossible level compared to what she and the group had been doing just a few days earlier.

Donald Roy, who worked as a participant-observer in a factory, describes the pressures against deviancy from the point of view of one who was the object of these pressures. Roy's job was paid on a piece-rate basis; the more he produced, the more he would earn (176, p. 23):

From my first to my last day at the plant I was subject to warnings and predictions concerning price cuts. Pressure was the heaviest from Joe Mucha, . . . who shared my job repertoire and kept a close eye on my production. On November 14, the day after my first attained quota, Joe Mucha advised:

"Don't let it go over $1.25 an hour, or the time-study man will be right down here! And they don't waste time, either! They watch the records like a hawk! I got ahead, so I took it easy for a couple of hours."

Joe told me that I had made $10.01 yesterday and warned me not to go over $1.25 an hour. . . .

Jack Starkey spoke to me after Joe left. "What's the matter? Are you trying to upset the applecart?"

Jack explained in a friendly manner that $10.50 was too much to turn in, even on an old job. "The turret-lathe

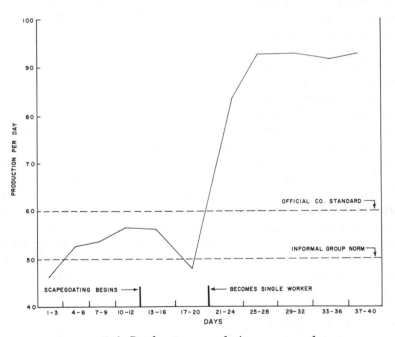

FIGURE 5–3. *Production record of one presser during a forty-day period.* (Adapted from 36, pp. 519–520.)

men can turn in $1.35," said Jack, "but their rate is 90 cents, and ours is 85 cents."

Jack warned me that the Methods Department could lower their prices on any job, old or new, by changing the fixture slightly or changing the size of the drill. According to Jack, a couple of operators . . . got to competing with each other to see how much they could turn in. They got up to $1.65 an hour, and the price was cut in half. And from then on they had to run that job themselves, as none of the other operators would accept the job.

According to Jack, it would be all right for us to turn in $1.28 or $1.29 an hour, when it figured out that way, but it was not all right to turn in $1.30 an hour.

Well, now I know where the maximum is—$1.29 an hour.

Some Questions about the Group in Organizations

The informal group in organizations poses a paradox: Groups can act with considerable effectiveness as law-enforcement agencies within the larger formal structure of the organization, but groups can direct the efforts of their members in opposition to organizational goals just as readily as they can direct members' efforts toward the support of these goals. This paradox caused students of organization to wonder how they might harness the power of the cohesive group. The answer seemed to lie in the approach taken by the Hawthorne experimenters in the relay-assembly test room, where the group worked toward the goal of efficient production. Why was the group so productive there and not in the bank-wiring room or on the shop floor?

Although part of the answer seemed to be the morale and job satisfaction—the "fun"—that the girls felt in the relay test room, job satisfaction alone is not the answer. Neither is the mere existence of friendly social relations and a tight-knit group. The results of the Hawthorne study suggested another element in the puzzle—namely, the friendly and permissive behavior of the test-room supervisor. We will therefore consider in the next chapters the role of the supervisor in the group, and some of the effects of supervisory behavior on the adjustments and performance of organization members.

chapter six

Supervision

What is supervision? One large company has formally defined supervision in terms of the following six requirements:

1. *Planning:* Make flexible plans regarding the work of subordinates. Make plans for self-development and development of subordinates.

2. *Organizing:* Make good use of allotted time. Be sure people reporting to you make good use of their time. Organize the job to be done in such a manner that the people doing that job clearly understand their responsibilities.

3. *Controlling:* See, through effective follow-up, that others do the job you have planned and organized.

4. *Communication:* Express yourself clearly and concisely in written or oral communication. Use good grammar. Keep the lines of communication open.

5. *Delegation:* Be receptive to duties delegated to you and be assured that duties delegated out are performed. Use good judgment in delegation. Do not delegate completely the responsibility of the job.

6. *Acceptance of Responsibility:* Accept the responsibility of your job performance and of the people reporting to you. Use good judgment in areas where responsibilities have not been defined and then take the responsibility for making decisions in these areas.

Formal statements such as this necessarily leave room for interpretation; no two supervisors would fulfill these requirements in quite
the same way. Furthermore, many aspects of the supervisor's work life
simply cannot be covered by specific instructions. But even if their
jobs were defined in much finer detail, supervisors would differ in the
ways they carry out their activities. How do supervisors in fact differ
in their approaches to leadership, and what do these differences mean,
if anything, for the reactions and adjustments of their subordinates?

The Ohio State Leadership Studies

In 1945, a concerted investigation into the effects of leadership
was launched by a group of social scientists at the Ohio State University.
As a first step, these researchers attempted to discover precisely how
leaders differ in their leadership styles, by giving questionnaires to
large numbers of persons, supervisors and subordinates alike, in a
variety of organizations. One questionnaire, administered to Air Force
bomber crews, contained 150 items, including the following (64, 68):

    a. He [the leader] makes his attitude clear to the crew.
    b. He rules with an iron hand.
    c. He makes sure his part in the crew is understood by
       members.
    d. He maintains definite standards of performance.
    e. He finds time to listen to crew members.
    f. He looks out for the welfare of individual crew members.
    g. He treats all crew members as his equal.
    h. He is friendly and approachable.

Respondents checked their answers on scales from "Never" to "Always."
After analyzing the data collected in response to these items, the
researchers discovered two distinct factors or dimensions of leadership.
These dimensions have subsequently been found in a wide variety
of organizations.

Initiating Structure and Consideration

The first dimension is called *initiating structure*. It is consistent
in large degree with the basic role of leadership as leadership is tra-
ditionally defined. Items *a* to *d* measure this dimension. A leader high

in this dimension "organizes and defines the relationship between himself and the members of his crew. He tends to define the role which he expects each member of the crew to assume, and endeavors to establish well-defined patterns of organization, channels of communication, and ways of getting jobs done" (64, pp. 42–43). Initiating structure implies a style of leadership consistent with the formal role description at the beginning of this chapter.

The second dimension is called *consideration*. It defines a style of supervision similar in a number of respects to that in the Hawthorne relay-assembly test room. Items *e* to *h* measure this dimension. It is "associated with behavior indicative of friendship, mutual trust, respect, and warmth in the relations between the aircraft commander and his crew" (64, p. 42). Leaders who appear authoritarian and impersonal in their relations with crew members are low in consideration, as measured by the questionnaire. Although this factor implies something about the degree to which the leader is considerate of his men, it does not imply that he is lax.

Leader Competence

What do initiating structure and consideration imply for how well the supervisor is doing his job? As a second step in their program of research, the Ohio State scientists asked supervisors to rate more than one hundred air-crew commanders (in two separate studies) on such criteria as technical competence, effectiveness in working with other crew members, performance under stress, conformity to standard operating procedures, and over-all effectiveness as combat crew members. The results showed that these effectiveness ratings correlated positively with initiating structure. At the same time, these ratings either correlated negatively or not at all with the measure of consideration. Thus, commanders who were judged competent and effective *by their own superiors* tended to be high on initiating structure and low or indifferent on consideration.

However, ratings of the commanders' proficiency *by their own crews*—obtained from more than eighty crews—correlated positively with consideration as well as with initiating structure. Moreover, indices of crew *morale* showed positive correlations with both leadership factors, although not as consistently with initiating structure as with consideration. Apparently, superiors judged crew commanders' competence primarily in terms of formal and traditional standards. Crew members, on the other hand, were less conventional in their evaluations; they experienced a high degree of satisfaction under "considerate" commanders, and they judged these commanders to be competent. The overall pattern of findings led to the conclusion *"that to select a leader who is likely to satisfy both his crew and his superiors, we do best by choosing an aircraft commander who is above average on both leader behavior dimensions"* (64, p. 64; italics in original).

Supervision and Worker Productivity

Researchers at the University of Michigan's Institute for Social Research took a different approach from that of the Ohio State group, although in a number of respects the results of their work overlap. These researchers administered questionnaires to female clerical workers in an insurance firm, white- and blue-collar workers in a power plant, railroad workers, and production workers in an earth-moving machinery company. They also interviewed supervisors. The researchers looked at high-producing work groups and those which were low, and they found that supervisors in these respective groups were often reported by their subordinates or by themselves to behave quite differently. Although the differences were not always significant statistically, many conformed precisely to what was suggested by the Hawthorne research; supervisors in high- as opposed to low-producing work groups acted like the supervisors in the relay-assembly test room (79, 80, 81, 82): They treated their men more like human beings, not merely like cogs in a machine or instruments for turning out a product. When confronted by subordinates whose work was poor, they looked for remedies or causes rather than punishments. Supervisors in low-producing groups, on the other hand, were likely to criticize subordinates whose work was poor and to exercise *close* rather than *general* supervision.

The pattern of results in these studies suggested a general principle underlying the behavior of the effective supervisors. Likert calls it the *principle of supportive relationships*: *"The leadership and other processes of the organization must be such as to ensure a maximum probability that in all interactions and all relationships within the organization each member will, in the light of his background, values, and expectations, view the experience as supportive and one which builds and maintains his sense of personal worth and importance"* (92, p. 103; italics in original). Supervisors, in other words, must support or help their subordinates achieve satisfaction for their ego and other motives in addition to the economic one.

In general, Likert's principle implies that (a) the supportive supervisor is sensitive to the needs and feelings of his subordinates; (b) he respects and trusts his subordinates; (c) he is receptive to their ideas and suggestions; (d) he has a sincere interest in the welfare of his men.

The supportive supervisor may express his interest in a variety of ways. He is helpful and friendly rather than hostile. He tries to prepare his men not only for their present jobs but for higher-level ones. The supportive supervisor is "considerate," to use the term of the Ohio State research. In the terminology of bureaucratic theory, he is *not* impersonal, although he is fair and impartial. The effective supervisor behaves in many ways directly contrary to the prescriptions of bureaucratic, administrative, and scientific management theories. He expresses warmth and human feeling and expresses them in ways that are sincere and personal. Furthermore, his judgments are always intended to serve the best interests of the employees as well as the company (92, p. 101).

The Michigan research also suggested that, in addition to being supportive, the effective supervisor differentiates his role from that of the worker; he plans, regulates, and coordinates the activities of his men but does not engage directly in the production tasks of the work group. These are basic supervisory functions, and they encompass much of what is meant by "initiating structure." Although the effective supervisor emphasizes his human-relations function, he does not abdicate his formal role of supervision; he does not act just like another member of the work group.

Table 6–1, from the study of railroad workers, illustrates this differentiation.

Supervision, Satisfaction, and Personal Adjustment

Some of the supervisory characteristics associated with high worker productivity are related to favorable attitudes and low absenteeism of subordinates. Mann and Baumgartel found in their study in a power plant that low absenteeism characterized groups where workers reported that the foreman (a) creates an atmosphere which contributes to free and easy discussion of work problems, (b) has time to talk to

TABLE 6–1. *Relation to section productivity of what foreman reports doing on the job.* (From 82, p. 14.)

	Planning; skilled tasks	Providing materials to men; Watching men	Same things men do	Keeping up track	Number of duties mentioned*	N
Foremen of High Sections	42	41	8	7	98	36
	83		15			
Foremen of Low Sections	25	42	15	14	96	36
	67		29			

* Responses total more than 72 because many foremen gave more than one answer.

his men about personal problems, (c) holds group discussions with his men, and (d) can be counted on to "go to bat" or "stand up" for his men.

But the effects of supervision may go beyond absenteeism and other indices of adjustment at work. They may extend into the personal lives of members even away from the job. Selvin asked Army trainees to describe their officers' behavior. He then categorized the trainees into three groups—those who were under (a) "persuasive," (b) "arbitrary," and (c) "weak" leadership climates. We shall describe only the first two climates, since the effects we want to discuss are greatest in them.

The *persuasive* climate approximates the more closely of the two the atmosphere of effective leadership which we have been describing. It includes the leader who takes an interest in his men, "goes to bat" for them, enjoys their confidence, and "is able to carry out the requirements of his role and still maintain good relations with his subordinates" (137, pp. 37–38). The *arbitrary* leader is low on these characteristics, is more harsh and oppressive, and is clearly nonsupportive.

Selvin expected that arbitrary leadership would generate tension and provoke attempts to relieve that tension. In order to test this idea, he asked the trainees how frequently they engaged in seventeen off-duty activities, such as reading, sports, attending chapel, eating between meals, getting drunk, blowing one's top, and fighting. He found that trainees engaged in thirteen of these activities more frequently under arbitrary leadership than under persuasive; whereas under the latter, trainees engaged more frequently in only two of the activities. Selvin concluded that the higher frequency of off-duty activity under arbitrary leadership was the result of greater stress and fewer opportunities for the release of tensions (137, pp. 87–88).

The Supervisor and the Group

The group, as we have seen in the previous chapter, is an important, if informal, locus of control within the organization. *Cohesive* groups especially are effective in mobilizing the efforts of members toward—or against—the formal goals of the organization. Theoretically, the objectives of the organization would be most significantly advanced if the social groups within it were highly cohesive and had norms representing high standards of performance.

Likert suggests that the supervisor plays a crucial role in achieving this combination. He proposes specifically that supervisors work to build their subordinates into cohesive work groups. If supervisors are also able to create positive attitudinal climates within these cohesive groups then the performance of members should be outstandingly high. Figure 6–1 illustrates this effect. It shows data from thirty-one geographically separated departments in a nationally organized company. These departments engage in comparable work and vary in size from about fifteen to more than fifty employees. Likert grouped them into four clusters according to the degree to which questionnaire responses of employees and supervisors conformed with the theoretical ideal: cohesive groups in which workers and supervisors have favorable attitudes toward each other. Thus, cluster 1, consisting of seven departments, is high on cohesiveness. In this cluster, workers indicate relatively high pride in their work group, a strong sense of belonging to the group, and favorable attitudes toward the other men. *At the same time,* supervisors and workers in this cluster indicate relatively favorable attitudes toward each other. The second cluster includes eleven departments in which work groups are relatively low in cohesiveness but mutual attitudes are relatively favorable. The third cluster includes eleven units which tend to be relatively low both on cohesiveness and mutual attitudes. The final cluster consists of only two departments, but these are interesting because they are *high* on cohesiveness and *low* on mutually favorable attitudes. The order of the clusters in their levels of productivity, as indicated in Figure 6–1, is consistent with the theory; cluster 1 is the highest, and 4 is the lowest.

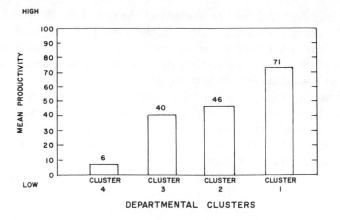

FIGURE 6–1. *Productivity of the different clusters of departments.* (From 92, p. 127.)

Some Questions About Research on Supervision

Results from a large number of such studies as the above seem reasonably consistent in showing that aspects of worker adjustment and performance are related to supervisory practices. Furthermore, much of this research supports the results of the Hawthorne study. It also raises a number of questions.

Supervisory Practice—Cause or Effect?

Are the adjustments and performance of subordinates the result or the cause of supervisory practice? One might argue, for example, that close, punitive supervision is the result rather than the cause of low productivity. Equally logical is the argument that such relationships are circular; supervisory practice has an effect on the adjustments and performance of workers which in turn affect the supervisor's approach to his job.

Experimental studies have an advantage over surveys in helping to settle arguments of this kind. One experiment by Day and Hamblin (41) is especially interesting because of its attempt to simulate, in the laboratory, industrial work groups under varying conditions of supervision.

Twenty-four groups, each consisting of four college women, were asked to engage in a task of assembling models of molecules with pegs and balls. The participants worked from elaborate blueprints but each group member specialized in one part of the task. Records of the number of correct connections made during a forty-minute work period were taken as the measure of productivity. Questionnaires measured aspects of the subjects' satisfactions in the work situation as well as their attitudes toward the experimental supervisors.

Two dimensions of supervision were introduced: close versus general, and punitive versus nonpunitive, permitting an investigation of four combinations of leadership: (1) general nonpunitive; (2) general punitive; (3) close nonpunitive; and (4) close punitive. Under the experimental conditions of *general* supervision, eight instructions were used by the supervisor to help define the job. Under *close* supervision, forty instructions were used. The supervisor also hovered and watched the workers closely, sometimes repeating instructions as a check-up. *Punitive*-style leaders made "sarcastic, negative, status-defeating remarks" as a means of punishment; but no such remarks were made under conditions of *nonpunitive* leadership.

Figure 6–2 shows the effects of these various styles of leadership on the productivity of group members and their aggressive feelings toward their supervisors. Both dimensions of supervision have significant effects. These results add credence to the contention that variations in supervisory style affect worker performance and adjustment; they do not, however, rule out the contention that supervisory style may also be a result of subordinate behavior. It seems reasonable to think that both arguments have validity. Supervisory style is both a cause and an effect of worker performance.

Some Complexities in the Effects of Supervision

A second question stems from some inconsistent results in the studies of supervision. Leadership practices that seem to produce high levels of subordinate performance in one situation may sometimes show no effect, or even a negative one, in another situation. The leadership process is complex; we are still far from understanding it fully and predicting its effects completely. One aspect of this complexity concerns the distinction between leadership *practices* and leadership *principles*. The same practice in different situations may represent quite different principles. For example, checking on the work of subordinates could imply close (nonsupportive) supervision in one situation, but help (support) in another, depending upon the nature of the job or the expectations of the persons involved.

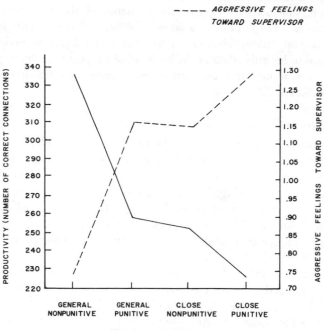

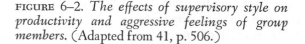

FIGURE 6–2. *The effects of supervisory style on productivity and aggressive feelings of group members.* (Adapted from 41, p. 506.)

A further complexity can be seen in the effects of one supervisory practice on another practice. For example, to be effective, a supervisor should be (a) friendly and (b) objective in relation to his subordinates. If the supervisor is too friendly, however, he may lose objectivity (34, 49). Similarly, the effects of one supervisory practice on subordinates' behavior may depend upon other practices of the supervisor. For example, supervisors who are supportive are likely to elicit high group-performance norms *only if they also encourage efficiency* (117). If they do not, supportiveness actually correlates negatively with group-performance norms. (Since most supervisors probably encourage efficiency, supportiveness is more likely to have a positive than a negative effect on production norms.)

Finally, the effects of a given supervisory practice may vary with the organizational conditions under which it occurs. One important condition, suggested by Pelz, is the influence of the supervisor in the organization (119). Unless a supervisor has influence with his own superiors, supportive behavior on his part is not likely to make much difference to his subordinates. What kind of support does "going to bat" for his men represent if the supervisor, because of little influence, always "strikes out"?

How to Change Supervisory Practice

A further question is raised by the leadership studies: How is it possible to get supervisors to behave in the superior ways suggested by this research? An answer that seemed reasonable to many psychologists is human-relations training. These psychologists supposed that the principles of effective leadership can be taught through discussions or lectures in classrooms. However, significant and permanent changes in supervisory practice as a result of human-relations training have *not* been found (33, 50, 65, 66, 101).

In general, although supervisors tested before and after the training sessions changed in their opinions about supervision, for some reason they did not (or could not) apply on the shop floor what they had learned in the classroom. Although these negative results do not prove that supervisory training is ineffective (perhaps the training was not properly done), training by itself is evidently not the answer. A study by Fleishman helps explain why.

Fleishman studied the results of a training program designed to change the attitudes and behavior of foremen on the Ohio State leadership dimensions, consideration and initiating structure. An opinion questionnaire administered to the trainees at the beginning and at the end of the training sessions showed that they did in fact change their attitudes in the expected directions, although not very much. Fleishman then studied four groups of foremen at varying times *after* training, and discovered that the amount of consideration which trained foremen showed, as judged by their own subordinates two to ten months after training, was *lower* than that of a comparable group of supervisors who had not undergone training. Fleishman concludes from this analysis that:

> The discrepancy between our results at the School and at the plant points up the danger of evaluating training out-

comes immediately after training. The classroom atmosphere is quite different from that in the actual work situation. Our results suggest that the foreman may learn different attitudes for each situation. The attitude that is "right" in the training situation may be very different from the one that "pays off" in the industrial environment (50, pp. 321–322).

Figure 6–3 represents a further step in Fleishman's analysis. Since essentially the same implications can be seen from the measures of

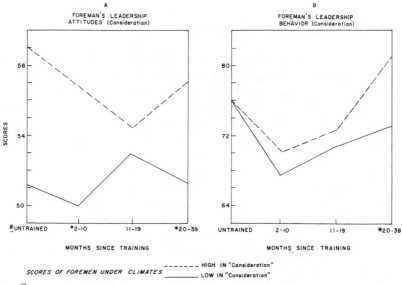

FIGURE 6–3. *Comparison of the leadership attitudes and behavior of foremen operating under different "leadership climates" back in the plant.* (From 50, p. 324.)

initiating structure only the data on consideration appear. Graph A shows the results of an opinion questionnaire designed to measure how the foreman thinks he should lead his work group. Graph B shows the results of a questionnaire administered to the foremen's subordinates, who described the foremen's behavior on the job. Four comparable groups of foremen are shown along the horizontal axes: (a) those who have had no training and (b) those who had been out of training two to ten months, eleven to nineteen months, and twenty to thirty-nine months, respectively.

In these graphs, the dashed lines represent the consideration scores of supervisors who themselves work under leaders high in consideration. The solid lines apply to supervisors who are subject to a leadership climate low in consideration. These differences in leadership climate, rather than training, seem to be the more significant determinant of supervisory style.

The Organization as a System

The research by Fleishman and that of Pelz, who demonstrated that the effects on subordinates of supervisory supportiveness depend on the supervisor's influence with those above him in the hierarchy, signaled an important change in the thinking of some psychologists. Formerly, psychologists assumed that the responsibility for supervisor-subordinate relations lay with the supervisor. Fleishman's and Pelz's studies called attention to the supervisor's supervisor and by implication to the supervisors above. They pointed to the full range of the organizational hierarchy, to the larger system, in which the first-line supervisor and his subordinates play only a small part. In many cases, the supervisor operates within an organizational framework that allows him little freedom of action. He cannot simply *choose* to behave toward his subordinates as he would like, however more effective his desired behavior may be. He is frequently under greater pressure and closer supervision than his own subordinates, and this hardly contributes to his taking a supportive approach with them. Furthermore, his subordinates may distrust him, because they distrust the company—perhaps justifiably. In some cases, more effective supervisory practices cannot be instituted unless there are thorough-going and profound changes in company structure and policy.

Psychologists entered the study of organizations stressing the importance of individuals and interpersonal relations, and minimizing by implication the importance of the larger organizational structure. The work by Pelz and by Fleishman helped modify this exclusively psychological view. Psychologists were being forced into an appreciation of the organization as a system. In describing retrospectively this transition in the thinking of their own research group, Tannenbaum and Sea-shore put it this way:

> Our research was leading us slowly but surely up the organizational hierarchy. It now seemed apparent to us that to get supervisors to behave in optimum ways, one must create conditions in the organization as a whole which make it possible and easy for the supervisor to behave appropriately. Upon further investigation we found that the supervisor who pressures his men may be following the example of a superior, and that some supervisors used pressure with subordinates because they believed their organization's norms required this. If it is desired to have supervisors treat their subordinates with consideration, to respect their men, it is not sufficient just to *tell* the supervisors to respect their men and to explain the rationale for this. Instead, it began to appear that the best way to get the supervisors to respect their men is *to make the men respectable;* that is, to change the organization in ways to give them some authority, responsibility, influence, control over significant aspects of their work life; to give them respectability. (160, pp. 6–7).

This notion is consistent in spirit with a number of studies on worker influence and participation, which we will discuss next.

chapter seven

Participation

"It is impossible to conceive of the existence of organization at all unless some person or persons are in a position 'to require action of others.'" Lyndall Urwick (166, p. 45) defined in this way the essential role of authority in organizations. We have described briefly in Chapter 1 the function of the authority system. Some further distinctions and definitions are now in order. We can start with the term, *control*.

Control is any process through which a person or group of persons determines (i.e., intentionally affects) what another person or group of persons will do. Essentially it means creating an intended change in the behavior of others—getting them to do something they might not otherwise have done. The term influence is sometimes used interchangeably with that of control. We speak of control (or influence) quantitatively; an individual may exercise a great deal of control over another in the sense that he intentionally creates many and important changes in the other's behavior. Or he may not affect very much of a change, in which case the amount of control is small. Control may operate specifically, as when a foreman defines how a subordinate will do a particular job. It may also be more general, as in the determination of organizational policies and actions. Control may be mutual, persons in a group each having some influence over what the others will do; or it may be unilateral, one person controlling and the others controlled.

The concepts of authority and of control are interrelated. Authority is simply the *formal right* to exercise control. These terms are also related to the concept of *power* which means the *ability or capacity* to exercise control. Like authority, power is a *potential* which may or may not be realized.[1]

The distinction between authority and control is central to many of the problems of organizational management because the formal right to exercise control (authority) does not always lead to the actual exercise of that control. A basic question, then, is how to convert formal authority into effective control. What, in other words, makes authority work? The traditional answer to this question has been "legitimacy," the *right* to exercise control, buttressed by coercion and its counterpart, reward. Persons in authority are in the position to hire or fire, to promote or demote, to raise or lower wages. These are the traditional bases of power or of control in organizations. They often work effectively, but they also frequently have unintended and dysfunctional consequences.

Participation is one approach suggested by the Hawthorne study to the problems of authority. In general, it refers to the formal involvement of members in the exercise of control, usually through decision making in group meetings.

Studies in Participation

An attic on the campus of the University of Iowa was the site in 1938 of a unique set of experiments conducted by Lewin, Lippitt, and White on democratic and autocratic leadership in children's play groups. Children at play hardly seem to provide the basis for understanding men at work, yet this study has been a model for a great deal of subsequent research, some of it extending right into the work organization itself.

Kurt Lewin, under whose general direction and inspiration this work was undertaken, came to the United States as a refugee from Nazi Germany. He combined a strong penchant for abstract theorizing with

[1] Authors do not always agree on the definitions of these terms. We cannot delve here into the technicalities of definition and of measurement which the interested reader will find discussed in great detail elsewhere (35). The definitions which we propose above are consistent in large measure with those of Mary Parker Follett: "Power might be defined as simply the ability to make things happen, to be a causal agent, to initiate change. . . . Control might be defined as power exercised as a means toward a specific end; authority as vested control" (109, p. 99).

an intense desire to apply the science of psychology in creating a better world. There is nothing so practical, he would say, as a good theory. *Democracy* was to him, a practical ideal which psychological theory and research might help us realize more fully.

> Have you noticed the peculiar mixture of desperate hope, curiosity and skepticism with which the newly arrived refugee . . . looks at the United States? . . . He is more than eager to believe in this "haven for the oppressed," to see with his own eyes a people who have the Statue of Liberty standing at the gateway of the country and "equality of men" as its law. Still, he cannot but hesitate at every step; he can't help but have his heart filled with the anxiety of a person who thinks that he soon will find out whether the world and its history has meaning aside from the eternal fight between hunter and hunted: Is democracy more than an empty proclamation, is it more than a phrase for politicians? Is democracy something "real"? Is there anything behind democracy but a word? (quoted in 175).

These are some of the questions and ideals which underlay much of Lewin's work. For better or for worse, they are shared by many psychologists who have studied participation in the laboratory and in "real-life" situations.

Participation in Children's Groups

Lewin, Lippitt, and White distinguished their experimental groups in terms of the way control was exercised within them (175). In the *autocratic* group, the adult leader determined the activities of the children by giving frequent orders. In the *democratic* group, the children determined in large measure what they would do and how they would do it. Decisions were arrived at through group discussion with the assistance and encouragement of the adult leader, who made suggestions and provided information.

The results of these experiments were not as simple as the proponents of democratic (or of autocratic) leadership might have hoped. As expected the autocratic atmosphere generated a higher degree of tension than the democratic, and, in general, the children preferred the latter type of leadership, although individual differences were apparent in the children's reactions to the same style of leadership. For example, one boy who had been brought up in an authoritarian family did *not* prefer the democratic group; furthermore, two reactions to autocratic leadership were noted: (a) apathy and dependence; and (b) frustration and aggression toward the leader. But differences in the behavior of the children when the leader was present, and when he was absent from the room, provided some of the most interesting contrasts. When the leader was present, the proportion of time spent in productive activity was higher in the autocratic groups than in the democratic. When he was absent, the level of constructive effort dropped markedly in the autocratic groups, but it hardly changed at all in the democratic. Thus the leader's presence made a great deal of difference to the relative success of the groups.

In these studies, the hope for the democratic approach lay in the more desirable psychological atmosphere which prevailed in the democratic groups and in the ability of these groups to sustain themselves constructively in the absence of a leader. One might speculate that the democratic groups were more durable—but this is only a speculation, and perhaps a prejudiced one. So let us follow the problem a little further.

Changing Attitudes and Habits

During World War II, certain popular food items, such as steaks and chops, were in short supply though beef hearts, sweetbreads, and kidneys were abundant. How might the government change basic attitudes and habits so that people would consume more of the latter, unpopular foods? Lewin and his students showed that housewives who participated in discussion groups that came to a consensus concerning the use of the less popular foods were more likely to make the change than were a comparable group who were lectured on the desirability of the change (89).

Lewin offered a number of explanations for the superiority of the discussion groups, but one of the most significant concerns the *power of the face-to-face group*. He argued that, contrary to common belief, single individuals are *not* more pliable than groups.

> . . . it is easier to change the ideology and social practice of a small group handled together than of single individuals. One of the reasons why "group-carried changes" are more readily brought about seems to be the unwillingness of the

individual to depart too far from group standards; he is likely to change only if the group changes. . . . As long as group standards are unchanged, the individual will resist changes more strongly the further [he is] expected to depart from group standards. If the group standard itself is changed, the resistance which is due to the relation between individual and group standard is eliminated (89, pp. 204, 210).

Because individuals are members of groups, attempts to change them—particularly when they are members of cohesive groups with relevant norms—are likely to be fruitless unless the groups themselves are attacked. In order to change attitudes and habits, one must work with the existing relevant groups, or create new ones.

Now, what implications do these experiments with children and housewives have for the work organization? An experiment in a textile plant in Marion, Virginia, helps provide an answer to this question.

Overcoming Resistance to Change

The Harwood Corporation, a manufacturer of pajamas employs a predominantly female work force, normally enjoyed good labor relations, except for a chronic difficulty stemming from the commercial necessity of making frequent changes in its products and in its methods of doing jobs. Employees intensely resisted these changes. Grievances were frequent among those affected by the changes, turnover shot up, efficiency dropped, and output restriction and strong feelings of hostility toward management grew whenever these changes occurred.

The experiment, conducted by Coch and French, was based largely on Lewin's concepts of *group dynamics* and concerned variations in democratic procedure. Four groups of workers were involved. The first was a control group, which underwent a modification of jobs in the usual way: the new jobs were timed, piece rates were set, and the workers were informed at a meeting that the changes would take place because of the competitive conditions. As usual, the time-study man carefully explained the new method and answered questions.

The second group employed a system of participation through representation. After this group had met and heard the need for the change presented as clearly and as dramatically as possible, the group members agreed that changes leading to greater efficiency could be effected without putting an additional burden on the workers. Management then presented a general plan, which provided that members select several operators to learn and help design the new jobs. These special operators met as a group and made many suggestions that were incorporated into the new methods. After they learned the new jobs, piece rates were set on the basis of how they performed. At a later meeting, these representatives explained the jobs to all of the workers and trained them in the new methods.

The third and fourth groups were relatively small. They received treatment similar to that of the second group, except that *all* of the members, not just representatives, helped to design the new jobs. The experimenters found it especially interesting "that in the meetings with these two groups, suggestions were immediately made in such quantity that the stenographer had difficulty in recording them" (36, pp. 521–522).

The results of these experiments showed that the control group, which had averaged about 60 units of production before the change, dropped to about 50, and, as expected, maintained production at this depressed level. The group that participated through representation dropped immediately after the change but recovered gradually, so that after about thirteen days it was back to 60 units. After thirty-two days, it was almost at 70. The "total-participation" groups did even better. They recovered much more rapidly, exceeding 60 units only four days after the change and going beyond 70 units shortly after that.

Two and a half months after these experiments, thirteen members of the control group were allowed full participation in a new change-over. Figure 7–1 shows the results of this variation. These workers, who had dropped from 60 to about 50 units as members of the control group, increased their production to about 70 units when permitted to participate in designing their new jobs.

The psychological consequences of the participative approach were equally convincing. Aggression toward management decreased markedly, turnover dropped to a minimum level, and a sense of identification with the work and with the company increased.

An Experiment on the Authority System in an Organization

Harwood, at the time of these experiments, was a relatively small organization employing about 600 persons. The experimental changes were relatively localized and easy to achieve administratively. In 1949, Morse and Reimer undertook an experiment that posed quite a different problem (113). These researchers were influenced by the Harwood ex-

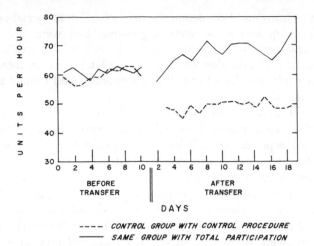

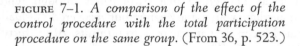

FIGURE 7–1. *A comparison of the effect of the control procedure with the total participation procedure on the same group.* (From 36, p. 523.)

periments, but their work diverged in important respects. The experiment took place in the home office of a nationally organized insurance company with many thousands of employees. The company conformed in important respects to the large bureaucratic model (although with some distinctly paternalistic overtones). Because of the massive and complex structure of the organization, the researchers were convinced that a localized, group-type experiment like that in the Harwood textile company would not be very helpful in understanding how participative methods might be applied within a complex organization of this kind. Therefore, the experiment they conceived encompassed a large segment of the organization hierarchy and was designed to test two contrasting systems of authority.

The experiment took place in a department employing approximately five hundred clerical workers and four levels of supervision. Throughout the course of the experiment, which lasted almost two years, the department continued to function as an integral part of the total organization, carrying out its normal function of processing records sent to the home office from agents around the country. The department was composed of four divisions, which were precisely parallel in type of work performed. In two divisions, an attempt was made to place a greater amount of control in the hands of the rank-and-file clerks, delegating to lower levels some of the decision-making authority of the higher levels. The vice-president delegated greater authority to the general manager of the department, who in turn delegated certain decisions to the division managers, and these managers in turn delegated decisions down the line, until clerks were in a position to make certain decisions that heretofore were made at higher levels. Through group meetings with their supervisors, the clerks made decisions concerning some of the work rules, vacation schedules, lunch hours and recess, overtime, and other matters of immediate concern to them. Furthermore, the supervisors were trained to help expedite this new system of control. Thus, appropriate training in human relations occurred together with significant structural changes. The two divisions which received this treatment comprised what the experimenters called the "Autonomy program."

In the other two divisions, called the "Hierarchical program," the control exercised by upper levels was increased. The methods of scientific management were employed and attempts were made, after studies and analyses of the work process, to make them more efficient. Decisions and policies were initiated at upper levels and passed down the line. These were sometimes explained through lectures by company officers.

The researchers expected to find the Autonomy program superior to the Hierarchical in productivity and in the psychological adjustments of employees, but the results did not conform entirely to their predictions. Company productivity records indicated significant improvement in *both* groups. Furthermore, the increase was greater in the Hierarchical divisions, where it averaged about 25 per cent; the Autonomy program averaged about 20 per cent. Like Lewin's autocratic children's groups with the leader present, the Hierarchical program did better in immediate performance. However, the experimenters recorded a number of changes which help define some of the psychological and organizational conditions under which the increases in productivity were achieved. Productivity increased in both groups, but for different reasons. First of all, the experiment provided documentation for the creation of significant and durable changes in supervisory practices. According to responses of the clerks to questionnaires administered at the beginning and at the end of the experiment about two years later, supervisors in the Autonomy program became more (a) informal, (b) psychologically close to their subordinates, (c) receptive to the clerks' ideas and suggestions, and (d) "general" (rather than "close") in their style of supervision. At the same time, supervisors in the Hierarchical program became more distant psychologically from the clerks.

Second, a number of changes in the clerks' adjustments and reactions accompanied the above changes in supervision. In the participative divisions, the clerks' feelings of self-actualization on the job and their general sense of satisfaction with the company increased, whereas the clerks in the Hierarchical program experienced an opposite reaction. The relationships among the clerks also changed. Sixty-one per cent of the girls in the Hierarchical program and thirty per cent in the Autonomy program reported at the end of the experiment that changes had taken place in their interpersonal relations. Table 7–1 contains a classification of the responses of those clerks who indicated that a change had taken place. These data make it clear that the social and psychological atmospheres were quite different in the two programs.

TABLE 7–1. *Changes in interpersonal relations among clerks as reported at the end of the experiment (per cent of respondents).*

CHANGE	AUTONOMY PROGRAM	HIERARCHICAL PROGRAM
More willingness to see other people's point of view, more friendliness	28	—
More cooperation, work better together	25	—
More tension, nervousness, fighting, jumpiness, biting each others' heads off, harshness; less kindness	16	35
Greater dissatisfaction, disagreeableness, friction; less cooperation	31	65
Total	100%	100%

Third, questionnaires administered at the beginning and at the end of the experiment indicated that the motivation underlying the productive efforts of the employees changed. The girls in the Autonomy program increased in their feelings of personal responsibility for the work and in their acceptance of company production standards. The Hierarchical divisions changed in the opposite direction, and the clerks here were more likely to express disapproval of high-producing coworkers. Thus, *opposition* and its motivational symptoms increased in the Hierarchical program but decreased in the Autonomy.

Theoretically, these changes in the clerks' reactions and motivations favored higher productivity in the Autonomy than in the Hierarchical divisions. Why, then, did productivity go up in both groups, and why did it increase at a greater rate in the Hierarchical program? Essentially, as a result of decisions to reduce the sizes of the work groups without reducing the volume of work, productivity was raised in both programs. However, the two programs differed crucially in how these decisions were made. In one program, managerial personnel made the decisions; in the other, the clerks and their supervisors made them. In the words of Morse and Reimer,

> The Hierarchically-controlled program [increased productivity] . . . by ordering reductions in the number of employees assigned to the tasks. Increases in productivity . . . were brought about as simply as that. This temporary increase . . . is not surprising and is traditional history in industry. In the Autonomy program [the increase in productivity] . . . was more complex but can be simply stated as follows. The Autonomy program increased the motivation of the employees to produce and thus they did not feel the need for replacing the staff members who left. . . . In addition, they were willing to make an effort to try to outplace some of their members in other jobs which they might like. The reductions in staff in the two programs came about in different ways. Those occurring by order in the Hierarchically-controlled program surpassed in number those occurring by group decision in the Autonomy program, but it is not clear how long the superiority of the Hierarchically-controlled program would have lasted (113, p. 128).

Thus, the advance in productivity in one program occurred because the clerks *wanted* to produce at a higher level; in the other, it occurred because the clerks *had to*. Therefore, the experimenters felt that the superiority of the Hierarchical program was at best a temporary one.

Some Tentative Conclusions about Participation

These experiments suggest that high levels of production can be achieved in different ways; there need not be just "one best way."

Traditional approaches, which include scientific management and hierarchical control, are clearly effective—although these methods may have social and psychological consequences that could eventually impede performance. Modifications of the traditional system of control that give workers some say in matters that affect them on the job can also be conducive to efficiency. This participative approach, which runs counter to traditional theory in significant ways, may be particularly effective in creating a work environment that is more rewarding psychologically to organization members. Furthermore, it is possible that the positive effects on organizational performance of this approach may be more apparent in the long run than in the short (93).

Although the evidence available is by no means conclusive, a larger role for workers in the decision-making processes within their organizations could lead to improved performance in some situations. Why has this approach not been more widely adopted? Part of the answer lies in *resistance to change*.

Management's Resistance to Change

Workers are by no means the only persons who oppose innovation in organizations; anyone is likely to resist a change that threatens or seems to threaten the loss of something he values. Managers are no exception and they have in general looked askance at plans to broaden the role of workers in decision making. Management's opposition to unions is in part an opposition to a change in the distribution of power in their organizations. This resistance has sometimes been irrational, since unions have been helpful to some managements in the difficult task of running their organizations (156).

There are a number of reasons, however, why managers oppose a more participative role by workers, whether through unions or as part of a more participative organizational system. First, traditional management theory makes no provision for worker responsibility or initiative—let alone control. Managers therefore learn ways of managing which preclude anything but a most limited and passive role for workers. Many managers express inconsistent views on this subject, however, since traditional approaches to management are opposed to generally held values about democracy. An international study of three thousand managers in fourteen countries showed that managers preponderantly endorse the *idea* of participative decision making. Nonetheless, most managers maintain that organization members are incapable of leadership, and that they prefer to be directed and to avoid responsibility. These inconsistencies imply the analogy of "a Jeffersonian democracy [built] on a basic belief in the divine right of kings. . . . The apparent enlightened democratic beliefs of managers with respect to organizational government are merely a superficial cover to basic negative beliefs about human capabilities" (63, p. 103).

Second, the experience of managers often supports the traditional rather than the participative view. For example, the traditional management approach may result in greater immediate productivity, as in the clerical experiment. However, this advantage in productivity may be exaggerated in the minds of managers who have no access to regular measurements (such as those in the clerical experiment) which record the relevant motivations, attitudes, and perceptions of the work force (92). Production figures may look good while the social and psychological atmosphere is deteriorating.

Third, managers fear that control by workers leads to chaos. Not only are employees considered incapable and poorly informed about important facts of organizational life, but they are often manifestly opposed to the company and its goals. Therefore, managers feel that placing power in the hands of workers would be disastrous. Ironically, participation may be most beneficial precisely where scientific management and other traditional approaches have led to opposition—as in the resistance to change at Harwood. Managers, however, are probably least receptive to the idea of worker participation under these circumstances.

Finally, managers prefer personally to be in a position of control, and they are likely to think that control by workers threatens their own power—and hence their self-interest. This belief is supported by two assumptions (154). The first has been called the all-or-none law of power; one either leads or is led, is strong or is weak, controls or is controlled. The second is the fixed-pie assumption of power. It argues that the amount of control exercised by members of a group or organization is a fixed quantity and that increasing the power of one individual (a worker) automatically decreases that of another (a manager). In the language of *game theory,* the distribution of power in a group or organization is represented by a zero-sum game. There are a number of reasons, however, for questioning these propositions.

Total Amount of Control in an Organization

Envision a graph in which the horizontal base represents the hierarchy in an organization, with the president at one end and the rank-and-file members at the other, and the vertical axis represents the degree of control that persons at the various hierarchical levels exercise. A curve plotted on such a graph will provide a rough, though meaningful, way of describing the distribution of control in an organization.

Tannenbaum and Kahn employed a graph of this kind in a study of four trade-union locals that differed in their effectiveness and in their levels of membership activity (158, 159). These researchers questioned members and officers about the influence that various persons and groups—the president, the executive board and the membership —exercised over decisions in the union. Curves were then drawn for each union on the basis of the responses to these questions.

The researchers found that the unions with active and influential members did not necessarily have uninfluential leaders. On the contrary, the curves for the two most effective unions showed that the members *and* the leaders exercised a relatively high degree of control. In these unions, both members and officers were relatively active; members attended meetings, took part in discussions (rather than just sitting and listening), and they communicated frequently about union affairs. Members and leaders influenced each other and, in the process, created effective action.

In the least effective union, on the other hand, a kind of laissez-faire atmosphere prevailed. Members and leaders were uninfluential compared to those in the effective unions; no one exercised much control. Tannenbaum and Kahn concluded that the effective unions were characterized by a greater amount of control than were the ineffective. A powerful membership apparently does not lead to weak leadership—nor vice versa.

This hypothesis relating the total amount of control and effectiveness in organizations has been investigated in a number of organizations with confirming results in most cases (15, 28, 118, 143, 155). Figure 7–2 shows this relationship among 31 geographically separated departments of a large industrial service organization. Each of the departments performs essentially the same work and careful records of productivity are kept by the company. Employees in these departments were asked the following question in a paper-and-pencil questionnaire: "In general, how much say or influence do you feel each of the following groups has on what goes on in your department?" Answers were checked on a five-point scale from "little or no influence" to "a very great deal of influence," for the following hierarchical groups: higher management,

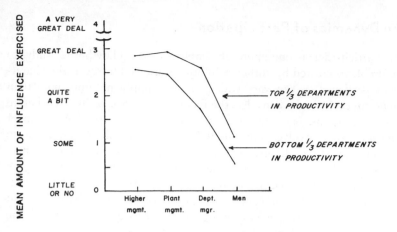

FIGURE 7–2. *Relation of department productivity to average amount of influence actually exercised by various hierarchical levels (as seen by non-supervisory employees).* (From 92, p. 56.)

plant management, the department manager, and the men. Figure 7–2 shows the average response to the above question for the one third of the departments highest in productivity and the lowest one third. The curve for the departments that were medium in productivity falls between those shown.

According to an analysis of these departments by Likert, "The high performing managers have actually increased the size of the 'influence pie' by means of the leadership processes which they use. They listen more to their men, are more interested in their men's ideas, and have more confidence and trust in their men" (91). These managers are more likely to interact and communicate with their subordinates through group meetings where they welcome opinions and elicit influence attempts. Suggestions which subordinates offer make a difference to the managers, and the subordinates are responsive in turn to their managers' requests. Furthermore, workers are members of cohesive work groups and at the same time mutual attitudes of workers and their managers tend to be favorable. Under these circumstances, influence by workers is not a threat to managers. On the contrary, it is part of a process leading to more effective organizational performance.

The Dynamics of Participation

Participation is one approach, implicit in the Hawthorne study, to the problems created by authority in organizations. However, the character of participation can vary widely. It may imply nothing more than a lone supervisor who considers the feelings and ideas of his men before making decisions, or it may refer to a formal and pervasive system of delegation that involves substantial influence for subordinates. Group meetings, for the exchange of ideas and the exercise of influence, may also be part of the process. But, essentially, it is a matter of some degree of control by subordinates over work-related matters.

Although different systems of participation will have different effects, participation generally mitigates if not overcomes some of the problems created by hierarchy.

Satisfaction and Personal Adjustment

Hierarchy creates sharp differences in the satisfactions and adjustments of persons at different ranks. Participation ameliorates this condition. In general, organization members *want* to exercise control, and they therefore find in participation an important source of gratification.

Members obtain several kinds of satisfactions from exercising control. The first is "psychological" or "symbolic." Individuals may derive satisfaction because of their need for self-determination or independence or power—or as a result of whatever satisfying meanings the exercise of control may have for them. It may, for example, imply to a member that he is important, or superior, or successful. In fact, individuals in positions of power often elicit behavior on the part of others which implies respect and consideration. Participation, in other words, can be ego enhancing.

Participation may also bring certain "material" or "pragmatic" rewards. A person who participates can make decisions and perhaps even affect policy in ways that are consistent with his own self-interest— depending on how far the participation scheme goes in giving power to members. Participative decisions are more likely than hierarchical decisions to take into account the needs and interests of all parties, so that control is less likely to seem arbitrary and disadvantageous.

Third, participation is often intrinsically satisfying; for example, it may consist of group meetings that discuss interesting topics and make important decisions. Furthermore, it may include challenging activities that draw upon intellectual, technological, and human-relations skills.

Workers may apply their knowledge and abilities to the development of new and better ways of doing their jobs. Not only is this a source of satisfaction, but it can be a source of many practical suggestions that contribute to efficiency, safety, or improved working conditions. Thus, participation may add to the complexity and skill of the job.

In sum, participation reduces some of the frustrations attached to positions of low rank. It does this by increasing the authority and status of these positions, by broadening the activities of these positions and by leading to decisions that seem less arbitrary and disadvantageous. It adds some of the qualities of the managerial role to nonmanagerial jobs. Participation, to some degree, brings workers into management. Thus, it affects more than their job satisfaction; it affects their motivation.

Motivation and Opposition

Hierarchy is divisive; it creates resentment, hostility, and opposition. Participation reduces disaffection and increases the identification of members with the organization. Individuals are more likely to feel some sense of commitment and responsibility relative to tasks that are brought before them in their capacity as decision makers. Supervisors no longer transmit communiques and orders unilaterally from above; the supervisor becomes someone to work with rather than against. Participation also encourages the exchange of feelings and ideas, thus reducing discrepancies in perceptions, ideals, and loyalties—discrepancies that exist characteristically between persons at different ranks and that may contribute to conflicts. Hostility and opposition are replaced by more cooperative attitudes, enhancing the influence which management has in its relations with subordinates. Paradoxically, *through participation management increases its control by giving up some of its authority.*

Control

One aspect of participation—an especially intriguing aspect because it is subtle and has not always been recognized explicitly—is its capacity to enhance the control exercised by managers while increasing that of rank-and-file members. This quality of participation is illustrated graphically in the control curves of Figure 7–2. March and Simon's discussion of "participative management" makes the point explicit:

> . . . where there is participation, alternatives are suggested in a setting that permits the organizational hierarchy to control (at least in part) what is evoked. "Participative

management" can be viewed as a device for permitting management to participate more fully in the making of decisions as well as a means for expanding the influence of lower echelons in the organization (104, p. 54).

Participation, far from being chaotic, can be a more orderly, integrated and controlled system than the traditional oligarchy. The nature of control and its distribution, however, are different. Control is more mutual rather than exclusively unilateral. Furthermore it is not intended to operate solely along the formal chain of command. *Peers* play an important part in exercising control and in maintaining adherence to organization standards which they have helped to establish. The face-to-face group is a vital element in this process. These groups, which might have had an informal existence in opposition to the organization are given formal status within the organization. Supervisors are integrated into the groups, and the groups' power is now exercised on behalf of the organization rather than in opposition to it.

Some Questions about Participation

A number of authors have raised serious questions about the generality and practicability of participation. For one thing, the logic of participation hinges on the very crucial assumption of a substantial commonality of interest between employer and employee (142). This assumption, you will recall, resembles the view of Follett and Mayo, but many persons have objected strenuously to it. The assumption may be more or less tenable, depending on political and economic circumstances. For example, it makes little sense in a nation occupied and exploited by a foreign power, and it is less tenable during an economic depression or a labor surplus than it is under prosperity or a tight labor market.

In the United States, the assumption of common interest has grown through the years. Labor leaders and labor intellectuals, who once had been vociferous opponents of this view, are now less inclined to argue against it. Some employers also have been opposed to the common-interest assumption, even though their public pronouncements have stressed harmony and agreement. But employers, like labor leaders, have through the years become more accepting of this assumption. The employer decides whether to allow participation in his organization, and (if he decides to allow it) whether it will be given an opportunity to prove or disprove itself. But, as Simon has put it, "the employer can tolerate genuine participation in decision making only when he believes that reasonable men, knowing the relevant facts and thinking through the problem, will reach a decision that is generally consistent with *his* goals and interests in the situation" (142, p. 111—italics in original).

Further questions have also been raised about some of the unfavorable by-products of participation—by-products that may limit its applicability. For example, group meetings solve some problems, but they also create new ones. Strauss has summarized a number of these:

> (1) individuals whose opinions have been rejected by the group may become alienated from it; (2) participation may lead to greater cohesion, but it may be cohesion against management; (3) participation may set up expectations of continued participation which management may not be able to satisfy; and (4) participation often takes a great deal of time, can be frustrating to those involved, and frequently results in watered-down solutions (151, p. 70).

The seriousness of such problems depends on a number of circumstances, including the human-relations skills and sophistication of organization leaders. The necessary skills are not now widely held. For example, the formal description of the supervisor's job (at the beginning of Chapter 6) says nothing about the supervisor's role as a leader of a decision-making group. Supervisors are not ordinarily expected to have this kind of capability. For participation to be successful, supervisors and managers will have to learn new styles of leadership. They will have to learn how to work effectively as "democratic-group leaders"; to accept influence from their subordinates and even to countenance, if not encourage, a questioning of their own ideas. Under a participative system, questioning by subordinates should not be construed as disrespect or insubordination, but rather as confidence, trust, and an interest in an effective organizational effort.

The expectations and ideology of the work force may represent further limitations on the applicability of the participative approach. An attempt to replicate the Harwood experiment in a Norwegian factory, for example, failed to yield the predicted results partly because of the different expectations held by the workers in this factory (52). Personality also affects members' reactions to participative control. In the Iowa experiments, one child who had been brought up in an authoritarian family stood out in his antipathy for the democratic approach. Vroom (168) found that differences in the performance of workers was a joint function of personality (whether authoritarian or egalitarian) and perceptions of the degree to which the supervisors were participative. Not all organization members react positively to participation.

Some final questions now deserve consideration. Social scientists have debated about the ethics of participation and the human-relations approach it represents. Is this approach bringing us an answer to the quest for a living democracy in the workplace? Is it a way of humanizing the workplace and of furthering the interests of all organization members? Or is it an attempt to sugarcoat a bitter pill, to disguise some of the harsh realities of organizational life and to manipulate workers and undermine their loyalty to their unions? (178, 179).

Perhaps we shall have a better basis for thinking about these questions after considering in the next chapter some specific applications of the research we have discussed so far.

chapter eight

Applications

The research and the ideas described in the preceding chapters are largely products of the academic mind. The implications of this work, however, are more than academic. One of the most exciting aspects of the organizational studies we have discussed is their application in industry. In this chapter we shall discuss several of these applications. Some of them have been developed by social scientists, others by engineers or administrators, and some have been inspired by political considerations. But all of them modify the classical views of organization so as to take the human factor more into account.

These applications differ along a continuum. Those at one end are primarily "psychological"; they focus on the individual members' personal conflicts, tensions, and frustrations, and are designed to help members adjust to their work situations. At the other end of the continuum are applications of a broader social or structural character, which imply a concern for the organization as a system. Unlike traditional bureaucratic and administrative theories, however, these applications assume important psychological effects consistent with the research we have discussed. The evolution of thinking and practice concerning human relations in organizations has followed an expanding course over the years from an almost exclusive emphasis on psychological techniques at one end of the application continuum to emphases that encompass applications of a structural kind.

Personnel Counseling

Personnel counseling was originally proposed by the Hawthorne researchers as the major concrete application stemming from their work. It seeks to improve the morale of workers and to help them adjust to their work situations.

The Hawthorne researchers looked on counseling as one of the solutions to human-relations problems after conducting a massive interviewing program in which workers were asked to describe likes and dislikes about their jobs. The researchers were impressed with the sense of relief and even satisfaction that many workers expressed after discussing their job problems. Typical comments were: "Gee, it's good to get this off your chest!" and "I surely enjoy a good talk like this once in a while. A fellow has to get rid of the gas some way" (124, p. 194). Having workers talk about their job problems seemed to be a way to improve the human-relations climate in a firm. This conclusion was consistent with the results of the relay-assembly test room, where the presence of a considerate and attentive observer seemed to improve morale. Since all the workers could not be brought into the test room, perhaps the test room could be brought to the workers, in the person of an attentive counselor.

The mechanics of counseling are relatively simple, though not uniform. In general, the counselor seeks out problems of human relations in the work situation, and he is available to all personnel when they feel the need of his services. A supervisor may approach the counselor because of a troublesome subordinate, or a subordinate may seek help because of difficulties with his superior. For example, a foreman may ask the counselor to consult with a worker who is frequently absent or late. The counselor will discuss the problem confidentially with the employee and try (a) to discover from what the employee says what the *real* basis of the problem is and (b) to help the employee discover what the real causes are. For example, discontent on the job may represent a basic dissatisfaction in the employee's home life, and the counseling discussion may, therefore, delve into questions of a highly personal nature. Maier cites as an illustration a man who blamed low wages and lack of recognition for his dissatisfaction at work when, in fact, his wife's homosexual tendencies were the basis of the disturbance (98, p. 416).

However, not all human-relations problems are related to employees' personal maladjustments. Roethlisberger and Dickson illustrate this with the hypothetical case of a hard-working girl who is dissatisfied with her job because she has not been given much chance to improve her position. The counselor in this case asks the girl whether she has discussed the problem with her supervisor. She has not, and the counselor focuses her attention on this possibility. The girl then takes the problem up with her supervisor, and the supervisor in turn discusses it with the counselor. This discussion helps the supervisor understand the work situation so that he can discuss the problem with the employee in a more rational and intelligent manner. The outcome is a happy one for both the company and the girl: "As a result of this process she goes back to work in better spirits. She is restored to her normal effectiveness and her efficiency may rise" (124, pp. 600–601).

It is also possible that the supervisor may make some changes in his own behavior or in the situation so as to help an employee adjust. The supervisor may find, for example, that a woman employee feels lonely and rejected, and he may therefore make an effort to give her extra attention (98, p. 419). Sometimes work routines can be changed so as to accommodate dissatisfied workers.

Counseling illustrates well the application of psychological principles in the industrial setting. It is an approach to problems of human relations which draws upon research in clinical psychology as well as upon research in industry. Counseling assumes a basic unity of interest and values between employees and management. According to this assumption, the tensions and conflicts in industry are due largely to faulty communications, misunderstandings, and maladjustments of workers, and counseling helps to correct these faults. It is recognized that factors in the organization—factors external to the worker and beyond his immediate interpersonal relations—may be the cause of difficulty, but the scope within which these faults can be analyzed and corrected is usually limited. In general, management policy and basic organization structure are not considered adjustable.

Survey Research

The Hawthorne researchers conducted a survey of workers' attitudes and perceptions in their search for data to be used in their supervisory training program. The need for facts about workers' attitudes is now widely felt by managers.

Survey research involves the systematic collection of information through interviews, questionnaires, or observation. The term *systematic* implies that the data collected represent the population under study within reasonable limits of error and are collected by trained personnel with an emphasis on objectivity.

Although survey data have been used to improve human relations in several ways, surveys are used most frequently to evaluate and implement management policies (76). For example, managers may want to find out whether employees read the company magazine, whether workers are satisfied with their jobs, or whether workers are satisfied with the company retirement plan. These surveys sometimes lead to changes. The company magazine may be made more attractive, or mailed to homes rather than handed out at the plant. One company, described by Kahn and Mann, changed its retirement plan as a result of a survey so as to accommodate new workers who had been excluded from the original plan. As a result of this change, along with a number of others suggested by the survey, the proportion of employees satisfied with the plan increased by about 30 per cent.

Survey data which are used in supervisory training programs (as in Hawthorne), or which are used to keep management better informed about the thinking of the work force, represent an aid to management in *expediting* company policy. Surveys may also be used to help *modify* policies, although this use is relatively uncommon. For example, Kahn and Mann report a company which was troubled by a lack of concern on the part of supervisors with production costs (76). A survey revealed that a supervisor's concern for such costs was affected by the extent to which he was involved in budget-setting decisions. These data suggested that supervisors should have had budget information that had been kept from them and should have shared responsibility for budget decisions. This suggestion implies a change in the distribution of power within the company hierarchy, and a modification, therefore, of company policy.

Like counseling, survey research in industry has generally been utilized for implementing rather than changing organization policies. Managers are usually reluctant to question the underlying policies of the organization or its structure. Employed in this limited way, survey research can make administration more efficient; but, in the long run, improving administrative efficiency may not represent the most constructive contribution to organizational effectiveness. It may even impede effectiveness, since it strengthens old policies that may have outlived their usefulness.

Sociotechnical Systems

Technology has important social and psychological effects. Mass production, for example, often breaks down jobs into their simplest components, which may frustrate the workers. Technology also affects relations between workers, sometimes preventing or impeding their communication with one another or their forming of social groups.

Psychologists have investigated redesign of jobs to take account of these social and psychological implications. Walker and Guest, for example, have noted several practical approaches to this problem (171). *Job rotation* is one approach. According to this system, workers learn several jobs which they can perform alternately, thus adding variety to their work. *Job enlargement* is a second approach. This method broadens the scope of a job to include several steps rather than one, in the total production cycle. In effect, job enlargement modifies the requirement that tasks be broken into their simplest constituent motions; two highly specialized tasks might be combined into a single, less specialized (and less monotonous) one. The enlarged task implies greater variety, allows more flexibility, requires increased skill—and it is likely to be more meaningful to most workers.

Psychologists at the Tavistock Institute in London have placed special emphasis on the *sociotechnical* implications of job design (45, 123, 164). These researchers propose that the most productive and satisfying work systems are those that combine social and technological considerations. In coal mining, for example, a system of cohesive teams, in which miners can support and help one another, has proved superior to the system in which workers were relatively isolated. The teams, however, should be set up so that their members share responsibility for a meaningful part of the mining task—and this is where technology imposes its limitations and defines what is possible by way of social interactions.

The sociotechnical approach is in some ways like that of job enlargement; recombining the simple, broken-down elements of a job into a larger whole. However, the reconstituted jobs are assigned to groups, not to individuals. The objective is to establish cohesive social units of workers and supervisors that correspond to meaningful technological units. The work groups should have reasonable autonomy and responsibility *as groups* for the total task. This matching of social and technological aspects of the work situation yields optimum results for the organization and its members.

The Training Laboratory

We have described in Chapter 6 some disappointing experiences with supervisory and managerial training. Partly as a result of these experiences, social scientists have been devising new, and what may prove to be more effective approaches to changing the human-relations skills of supervisory and managerial personnel. These new approaches to training differ from earlier methods in several ways. First, they attempt to work on an emotional as well as an intellectual level. They are concerned with changing the behavior of trainees through affecting their basic attitudes toward themselves and others. Psychologically, this process is a deeper and more intensive training experience than that of older methods.

Second, these new approaches focus on *the group*. The creation of a cohesive training group, one that is important to members and therefore exerts strong forces on them, is frequently a prime requisite.

Third, such training is not addressed so much to changing specific traits as it is to changing very general orientations and values. It attempts to make people more concerned about and sensitive to human relations; it tries to build understanding and general interpersonal competence.

Finally, training programs may be part of a concerted effort to change values and behavior in a coordinated manner throughout important segments of the organization—not just at the supervisory level. For example, a training program may start at the top of the organization and proceed downward, so that the training is more *extensive* organizationally and more *intensive* personally. The program may be addressed as much to creating changes in the total character of the organization as to creating changes in individual members (see, for example, 10, 23, 24, 139).

The term *training laboratory* refers to such a coordinated program. Lectures and various exercises such as role playing in group situations may be employed as part of the program, but the core of the training laboratory is usually the *T-Group*.

The T-Group and Sensitivity Training

There is some variation in the way T-Groups are run, and in their specific objectives.[1] *T* stands for training, and this implies as the major general objective, *learning* on the part of trainees. This objective is usu-

[1] The material on the T-Group is drawn primarily from Bennis (20), Bradford et al. (29), Marrow (105), Seashore (133), R. Tannenbaum et al. (161), and from my own experience as a participant in T-Groups.

ally translated into several more specific ones: A trainee should acquire more understanding of himself and others, of his own motivations and feelings, and of the effects of his behavior on other people; in other words, he should become more sophisticated about interpersonal relations and group processes. This increased sensitivity should increase the trainee's skill in interpersonal relations and increase his capacity to be helpful, considerate, and supportive toward others. It should help him be a more effective communicator and more constructive in exercising influence within a group. The T-Group is also likely to encourage him to be a more democratic leader since the encouragement of "democratic" or participative leadership and decision making has been implicit as an aim in many T-Group training programs.

The T-Group is a unique kind of discussion group composed of approximately ten persons. Members may be complete strangers, or they may be co-workers. The uniqueness of the T-Group can be seen in a number of characteristics. It is *leaderless and unstructured*. Although a professional trainer is usually present, he is likely to be *non-directive;* that is, he does not tell the participants what they should discuss, and he tells them only minimally how they should proceed. He may, however, help clarify what is happening in the group, or provide factual information.

The atmosphere, then, is *permissive* in that the participants can in principle do what they like. This means they can *experiment;* they can engage in behavior that is new to them, which they might like to "try on for size." For instance, a passive person might try being ascendant or aggressive, to see what effect he has on himself and on others. An inhibited person may say things that he would not dare say elsewhere. The T-Group is set up to encourage such experiments, and the members come to understand their value. The T-Group therefore provides a social structure in which ordinary rules of propriety are suspended and where the participants can define their own limits.

The T-Group is concerned with itself; it is *self-analytic*. The members turn in to the group for the subject matter of their discussion. In doing this they inevitably talk about themselves and, ideally, they discuss themselves openly, describing in some depth their pertinent feelings and motivations. But a member does not talk only about himself; he offers his reactions about other group members. The value of the personal experiments depends on this *feedback,* so that a member who ventures into action in the group can learn from the others what the effects of his behavior may be. Is he "coming across" as he thinks or as he wants to?

These characteristics of the T-Group, the lack of structure, the permissiveness, the experimentation, the self-analysis and feedback have some profound effects. For example, the initial lack of structure and the consequent ambiguity of the situation arouse *anxiety*. Members are not sure what is likely to happen. They do not know whether the discussion will focus on them, will get dangerously personal, or will lead to threats or fights. They do not know how much of themselves they should expose. Participants, therefore, approach the group with trepidation. They may feel insecure, nervous, distrustful, impatient, resentful toward the trainer; and they are worried about expressing these untoward emotions. Some members may try to create structure in the group by assuming leadership, and conflicts arise out of such attempts. These more or less intense emotions and the interpersonal relations they generate become grist for the analytic mill.

The ambiguity and the emotion generated by the group session lead members to question implicitly if not explicitly their own motives. Long-standing values of members do not seem to apply or to make sense in the new and strange situation. These values are therefore "unfrozen," to use the term of Lewin (88), and this unfreezing sets the stage for change. The following example, taken from a group of managers, is an illustration of how feedback contributes to the change:

> "Ken, you intimidate me," says Charles. "You get sarcastic. You sulk when anyone disagrees with you. When you walk into the room, I feel like standing at attention and saluting. I wonder if your employees feel that way."
> Ken answers, "I certainly don't want them to."
> "Don't you?" Charles continues. "I wonder if you really know how you want them to feel. And I wonder if you know as much about what's going on in your company as you think you do" (105, pp. 40–41).

An essential element in this process is the development of a cohesive group and a sense of intimacy among members. Members become attracted to and dependent on each other; they turn toward each other for affection, support, approval. The group becomes a frame of reference; members are sensitive to and affected by it, and the group, therefore, is important in leading members to change, or, as T-Group theory puts it, to "grow."

Role playing may be employed in conjunction with the T-Group as part of a training laboratory or it can be used independently. Essentially, a play is performed in a group situation. The trainees are the actors, but they do not have a script; they make up their lines as they go along.

The process is initiated by a description of the situation to be enacted, and roles are assigned to the participants. For example, a supervisor may be asked to play the role of a union steward in a case involving a worker grievance. The character and background of the grievance are described to the player, and some of the conditions of the steward's life are specified, including perhaps his age, seniority, experience, skill, and friendships in the plant. The role player is asked to engage in the skit as if he personally were the steward under the given circumstances.

The participants learn their roles, and the play begins with the participants ad libbing their lines as they go along. Although this game may seem difficult and artificial, experience with the method leads Maier, Solem, and Maier (100) to conclude that "all people are good actors when they make up their own lines." The participants soon become involved in their roles.

The exercise is observed by other members of the training group, who engage with the role players in an analysis and evaluation following the performance. This group discussion is an integral part of the process and it contributes importantly to the learning and to the attitude changes that may take place.

The training laboratory—particularly the T-Group method—has aroused considerable controversy (116, 177). Critics deny, for example, that the T-Group creates lasting change in attitudes and values; some argue that unanticipated and undesirable effects may result from the highly emotional and volatile nature of the method. Unfortunately, the research documentation on these points is not entirely clear, but there is some indication that the effects may be more than temporary (67, 146). Furthermore, the number of people in industry who are convinced of T-Group effectiveness is growing.

The success of the laboratory method in a company probably requires participation in the laboratory of many if not all levels of management so that the changes in attitudes and behavior are induced widely. Top management must support the changes, and must be willing to structure their organization on a more participative basis. One of the objectives of the T-Group and of role playing is the development of skill for effective membership in decision-making groups. A potential of these methods can therefore be realized when they are used in conjunction with the systematic introduction of discussion and decision-making groups within an organization.

Participation Techniques

The desirability of more widespread participation in decision making has received some impetus from research, as we have seen in Chapter 7. While the conclusions drawn from this work are not above controversy, an increasing number of industrial leaders are convinced that worker participation can contribute to more effective industrial performance. Support for participation has also grown out of some of the prevailing social and political values of society. Practical schemes have therefore been formulated through which increased participation might be achieved. Some of these, which we have chosen as illustrations below, imply only a small degree of influence for rank-and-file members; others are more ambitious. All, however, represent workable approaches to enhancing the influence of lower-level personnel in organizations.

Work Simplification

The method known as work simplification is of special interest because it successfully unites the "scientific management" and "human relations" approaches. Work simplification is premised on the notion that workers are capable, along with supervisors and engineers, of designing new and more efficient work methods. It was created by Alan Mogensen to improve the design of tasks through drawing upon the knowledge and expertise which workers have about their jobs. But it is concerned as much with the *acceptance* of new methods as with creating them, for, as one advocate of work simplification has put it, "Too many systems for improving operations overlook the fact that a good method isn't a good method unless the operator thinks it is."[2]

Although work simplification encourages employees to contribute ideas about the work, it differs from the usual suggestion-box scheme. First, it is a *group* activity, not an individual activity. Participants in work-simplification teams meet together to discuss a work project and to create jointly a new and superior way of doing an old and inefficient job. Second, the participants are trained in the methods of work simpli-

[2] William T. Short, quoted in *The Wall Street Journal*, Dec. 8, 1959.

fication, including some principles of time-and-motion study; workers do not plunge into work simplification without indoctrination. Third, work-simplification teams have official status in the company. They have the sanction if not the active involvement of top management, and they can draw upon company facilities in their analyses and deliberations. Finally, the group activity is organized, so that work simplification teams approach their tasks in orderly steps (57).

They first select a job to improve. When a work simplification team is formed the initial tasks chosen might well be those which are outstanding candidates for improvement: bottlenecks, jobs which entail a lot of walking, high-cost operations, and those which are noted for giving trouble. As the group becomes more practiced, it will choose less obvious, but perhaps more rewarding opportunities for improvement. A second step is to get the facts. Participants may obtain blue prints, cost and production figures, sales records, samples, etc. They may also take motion pictures of themselves as they run through a job. This gives them a detailed view of how the task is performed. It is also personally rewarding, and participants may even borrow a projector to show the films at home. They then develop a solution and finally the improvements are installed. Personnel whose services are required for the installation will be brought in at this final stage, if they have not yet participated. Thus, every effort is made to involve all relevant people, engineers, accountants, supervisors, workers, who are affected by the change, or who may contribute to its success.

Work simplification shares some of its features with several other participation schemes, including the *Scanlon Plan* (85). This plan involves departmental production committees through which employees can participate in solving production problems. The Scanlon Plan includes a bonus system tied to improvement in efficiency. The details of this profit-sharing scheme are decided through joint participation by employee representatives and managerial personnel—as is the ultimate acceptance of the plan.

Work simplification and related schemes illustrate the possibility of combining some of the features of "scientific management" and of "human relations." One approach need not entirely preclude the other. A large number of testimonials from companies where work simplification has been adopted indicate a high degree of success, both in terms of efficiency and worker morale.

Participation and the Appraisal System

Work simplification shows how participative methods may be applied to what has ordinarily been considered a technological question; the application of participation to managerial appraisal illustrates its use in a *personnel* area.

In many companies, managers and supervisors are appraised annually by their superiors. Typically, the superior enumerates the subordinate's successes and failures during the past year and suggests ways in which the subordinate might improve. The superior may set future goals for the subordinate, and these goals may provide the basis for the next year's evaluation. This yearly appraisal has several objectives. It informs the person where he stands, it provides the basis for his raises and promotions—and it should contribute to an improvement in his performance. Unfortunately, it does not always have the desired effects, since it arouses anxiety and defensive behavior on the part of the person being evaluated. Nor is it conducive to objectivity on the part of the superior either, since it is emotionally charged. The subordinate may therefore leave the interview without having learned much, and may resist behavior changes that could lead to improvements (97).

Some companies are turning to other, more participative methods of appraisal. One organization, for example, has adopted a system in which the subordinate is asked to formulate his own performance goals (46, 53). These goals and the methods by which the subordinate hopes to achieve them are discussed with superiors in an atmosphere of mutual influence.

Maier has proposed a problem-solving approach to appraisal interviewing. The superior does not play the role of judge but that of helper (97). The main purpose of this approach is to stimulate development in the subordinate. The superior in this case does not propose problems or goals for the subordinate; rather, he attempts to stimulate the thinking of the subordinate, and he is willing to consider the subordinate's ideas. The appraisal interviewer uses questions not to point out weaknesses or errors, but to help the subordinate evaluate *his own* ideas and to formulate *his own* plans. Thus, the subordinate plays a more active, participative role in the appraisal process.

Organizational Families and Survey Feedback

Like the training laboratory, *survey feedback* is designed to induce changes in organizations, by changing individual attitudes and behavior and by establishing a new set of groups and working relationships which are conducive to heightened levels of participation throughout the organization (101).

Feedback involves several phases. First is a survey designed to measure the attitudes and perceptions of all organization members concerning their work, their superiors, peers, opportunities for promotion, and other aspects of their work situations. Then discussion groups are formed throughout the organization. Each group, called an *organizational family*, consists of a supervisor or manager and his immediate subordinates. Thus most supervisors and managers are members of two organizational families, one in which they are supervisors, and one in which they are subordinates along with their peers. These groups overlap as a result of the supervisors' joint memberships, and they form the crucial units of the feedback process.

The survey data are now "fed back"; that is, they are reported in these groups, starting with the group composed of the head of the organization and his immediate subordinates and moving gradually to lower levels. Since most supervisors are members of two "families," they will be exposed to the data first in the group where they are among their peers, and then in groups with their own subordinates. Thus, supervisors play a coordinating role between groups by carrying information from one group to the others.

The data are considered by each group. For example, the group members can compare the attitudes and perceptions of the employees in their own department with those of the rest of the company. Specific workers' dissatisfactions revealed by the survey data may form the basis for detailed discussion. Or data may reveal to supervisors that they differ from their subordinates as a group in the way they see important aspects of the work situation (see, for example, Tables 4–1 through 4–4). These data provide a springboard for discussion and interpretation, first among the supervisors as a group, and subsequently between supervisors and their subordinates. Since the data touch "close to home," the discussion may provoke some tension. Group members are therefore likely to start with relatively innocuous issues and move gradually into more sensitive areas such as their own conduct as supervisors. Through these meetings, organization members at different levels come to influence each other's understanding of the social and psychological problems in the organization. Ultimately the groups decide on courses of action to overcome these problems.

The feedback process is designed not only to solve immediate problems but also to establish a more permanent participative decision-making system for the organization. The total feedback process helps to develop group and interpersonal skills among members of work teams, so that they are better equipped to work together on problems that arise in the future. Furthermore, the network of groups and relationships which is created becomes a *modus operandi* for the organization; the tight-knit family groups, together with overlapping memberships (through supervisors), constitute a highly integrated organization structure, which is conducive to mutual influence among members and broad participation in discussions. It remains for the organization leadership to encourage the use of these overlapping groups by delegating to them decision-making authority concerned with work and organizational problems.

Feedback has been tried successfully in several companies although like the training laboratory it is still experimental.

Decentralization

The system of overlapping organizational families provides a basis for dispersing decision making throughout the organization rather than concentrating it at the top. This is one of the objectives of decentralization. The need for decentralization is especially great in large companies where size accentuates the problems of bureaucracy and authority. For example, large organizations suffer greater problems of morale than do small ones (1, 122).

Some systems of decentralization allow large organizations to maintain many of the economic advantages of bigness without suffering all of its social and psychological disadvantages. The Sears Roebuck Company, for example, achieves decentralization in two ways (180). First, significant authority is formally delegated to the local managers of the many stores around the country. (Although the wide geographic dispersion of the Sears stores encourages this policy, organizations need not be dispersed to be decentralized.) This policy places decision making close to the personnel responsible for carrying out the decisions, so that local personnel can handle practically all the problems of day-to-day operations without having to clear their decisions with central headquarters.

The formal delegation of authority, however, is not considered sufficient to assure effective decentralization. Sears, therefore, reinforces its policy directives with a special decentralization strategy, which has developed a very "flat" organization structure (see p. 10), with only four levels of supervision between the bottom and the top. A flat structure in an organization with well over a hundred thousand members has dramatic implications for "span of control" (see p. 10). It means, for example, that most executives have so many subordinates that they cannot possibly supervise them closely; executives must allow subordinates considerable leeway if the organization is to function at all. The flat structure of the Sears organization thus reinforces the company's policy directives; together they help assure effective decentralization.

Participation through Representation

Systems of worker representation, including those known as "joint consultation" and "workers' councils," have proliferated in a number of European countries since World War II (43, 44, 84, 110, 153). Unlike most of the applications we have described so far, these systems are largely the result of political developments. They are addressed in part to the problems of worker morale and motivation, and they illustrate an approach to participation which social psychologists are beginning to study.

The methods of joint consultation and of workers' councils vary from place to place, but each is a means for employees to exercise some organizational control through representatives. In Norway and in Germany, for example, workers' representatives are elected to the Boards of Directors of some companies. Workers' councils, composed of employees elected by the work force, have been introduced into organizations in Belgium, France, Germany, Poland, and Yugoslavia. These councils meet about once a month to discuss issues which come before them. In some cases, their function is only advisory; they make recommendations which management may accept or reject. For example, the German system, which goes as far as any in Western Europe, provides for an advisory function on financial and technical questions—although the German councils have considerable authority over vacation schedules, the discharge of workers, and their assignment to jobs.

The system in Yugoslavia is perhaps the most dramatic in its delegation of significant power to the councils. In theory, the councils are the final authority on many basic decisions, such as setting prices of products and allocating profits (that is, whether profits should be distributed as bonuses among workers or plowed back into the firms as capital investments). Councils are also concerned with hiring, firing, and disciplining workers. On occasion, workers' councils have fired managers.

Systems of joint consultation and of workers' councils are in their infancy but they seem destined to become an important part of industrial management in many countries. As of the moment, these systems have not entirely fulfilled their charters; the councils do not, in fact, exercise the control they are intended to exercise—sometimes because of the resistance of managements where workers' councils are installed. In Belgium, for example, the councils are supposed by law to run the company social-welfare programs. However, some employers have circumvented the councils by eliminating the welfare programs or transferring them to independent corporations (110). In Yugoslavia, managers—because of their administrative, political and technological expertise—are usually more influential than the councils, despite the legal supremacy of the latter. However, the councils are not entirely without influence.

A further question concerns the immediate impact of the representative system on the work lives of employees. To many workers, representation may not seem to change their daily routines very much—if at all. The frustrating aspects of technology and of bureaucratic administration remain pretty much the same. Although employees may perceive that the councils or boards of directors exercise significant influence in their organizations, they do not see themselves as sharing much of this influence. Psychologically at least, participation through representation lacks some of the important qualities of direct participation.

A Final Question

We have described some of the practical applications of social research in the work organization. The applications differ widely, but they need not be opposed to each other. Systems of decentralization, for example, can benefit from training programs which help participants become more competent in interpersonal relations and group processes. Workers' councils might be supplemented by systems of organizational families which allow employees to exercise influence more directly within their organizations. Work simplification and sociotechnical arrangements, survey research, feedback, and counseling can also contribute jointly to improving the human-relations climate of an organization.

The broad range of applications illustrates the potential of social research in industry, but the prospects are not always viewed optimistically by observers of the industrial scene. Some critics have warned that social science has been, and will continue to be, applied in ulterior ways to control the lives of organization members. Trade unionists have sometimes argued that social research is used to reduce the loyalty of workers to unions. There is some truth in these allegations. Nonetheless, it is essential that we understand the principles of human relations if we are to improve the human quality of organizations. Social science can contribute to this understanding, and social scientists, many of whom are committed to a belief "in the dignity and worth of the individual human being," will inevitably help formulate new techniques of application (7, 96). Not all of these applications will be effective, and some may not be worthy of the ideals professed by their creators. Yet it would seem that the *variety* of approaches to application which we have described illustrates a potential out of which much good can be extracted.

What do you think?

References

1. Acton Society Trust. *Size and morale*. London: Acton Society Trust, 1953.

2. Adorno, T. W., Frenkel-Brunswik, Else, Levinson, D. J., and Sanford, R. N. *The authoritarian personality*. New York: Harper, 1950.

3. Allport, F. H. Individuals and their human environment. *Proc. Ass. Res. nerv. dis.*, 1933, *14*, 234–252.

4. Allport, F. H. *Social psychology*. New York: Houghton Mifflin, 1924.

5. Allport, F. H. Teleonomic description in the study of personality. *Char. and pers.*, 1937, *5*, no. 3, 202–214.

6. Allport, G. W. *Personality, a psychological interpretation*. New York: Holt, 1937.

7. American Psychological Association. Ethical standards of psychologists. *Amer. Psychologist*, 1963, *18*, 56–60.

8. Arensberg, C., Barkin, S., Chalmers, W., Wilensky, H., Worthy, J., and Dennis, Barbara (Eds.). *Research in industrial human relations—A critical appraisal*. New York: Harper, 1957

9. Argyris, C. *Integrating the individual and the organization*. New York: Wiley, 1964.

10. Argyris, C. *Interpersonal competence and organizational effectiveness*. Homewood, Ill.: Dorsey Press, 1962.

11. Argyris, C. *Personality and organization*. New York: Harper, 1957.

12. Asch, S. E. The effects of group pressure upon the modification and distortion of judgments. In (95) pp. 174–183.

13. Atkinson, J. W. (Ed.). *Motives in fantasy, action, and society*. Princeton, N.J.: Van Nostrand, 1958.

14. Atkinson, J. W., Heyns, R. W., and Veroff, J.   The effect of experimental arousal of the affiliation motive on thematic apperception. In (13).

15. Bachman, J., Smith, C., and Slesinger, J.   Control, performance and satisfaction: An analysis of structural and individual effects. *J. pers. soc. Psychol.,* 1966 (in press).

16. Back, K.   The exertion of influence through social communication. *J. abnorm. soc. Psychol.,* 1951, 46, 9–23.

17. Baritz, L.   *The servants of power.*   Middletown, Conn.: Wesleyan Univ. Press, 1960.

18. Barkin, S.   Trade union attitudes and their effect upon productivity. In L. R. Tripp (Ed.).   *Industrial productivity.*   Madison, Wis.: Industrial Relations Research Association, 1951.

19. Bass, B.   *Leadership, psychology and organizational behavior.*   New York: Harper, 1960.

20. Bennis, W. G.   Goals and meta-goals of laboratory training.   In W. G. Bennis, E. H. Schein, D. E. Berlew, and F. I. Steele (Eds.), *Interpersonal dynamics, essays and readings on human interaction.* Homewood, Ill.: Dorsey Press, 1964, pp. 692–698.

21. Berlyne, D. E.   *Conflict, arousal and curiosity.*   New York: McGraw-Hill, 1960.

22. Birch, J. D., and Veroff, J.   *Motivation.*   Belmont, Calif., Wadsworth Publ. Co., 1966.

23. Blake, R. R., Mouton, J. S., Barnes, L. B., and Greiner, L. E.   Breakthrough in organization development.   *Harvard Bus. Rev.,* 1964, 42, no. 6, 133–135.

24. Blake, R. R., Mouton, J. S., and Bidwell, A. C.   The managerial grid.   *Advanced management office executive,* 1962, 36.

25. Blau, P. M.   *Bureaucracy in modern society.*   New York: Random House, 1956.

26. Blauner, R.   Work satisfaction and industrial trends in modern society.   In W. Galenson and S. Lipset (Eds.), *Labor and trade unionism.*   New York: Wiley, 1960.

27. Bonini, C. P., Jaedicke, R., and Wagner, H. (Eds.), *Management controls: New directions in basic research.*   New York: McGraw-Hill, 1964.

28. Bowers, D.   Organizational control in an insurance company.   *Sociometry,* 1964, 27, no. 2, 230–244.

29. Bradford, L. P., Gibb, J. R., and Benne, K. D. (Eds.).   *T-group theory and laboratory method.*   New York: Wiley, 1964.

30. Brayfield, H., and Crockett, W. H.   Employee attitudes and employee performance.   *Psychol. Bull.,* 1955, 52, no. 5, 396–424.

31. Brennan, N.   *The making of a moron*.   New York: Sheed & Ward, 1953.

32. Burns, T., and Stalker, G. M.   *The management of innovation*.   London: Tavistock Publications Ltd., 1961.

33. Canter, R.   A human relations training program,   *J. appl. Psychol.*, 1951, *35*, 38–45.

34. Carp, F. M., Vitola, B. M., and McLanathan, F. L.   Human relations knowledge and social distance set in supervisors.   *J. appl. Psychol.*, 1963, *47*, 78–80.

35. Cartwright, D.   Influence, leadership, control. In J. G. March (Ed.) *Handbook of organizations*. Chicago: Rand McNally and Company, 1965, ch. 1.

36. Coch, L., and French, J. R. P., Jr.   Overcoming resistance to change. *Hum. Rel.*, 1948, *4*, no. 1, 512–533.

37. Copley, F. B.   *Frederick W. Taylor*.   New York: Harper, 1923.

38. Crozier, M.   *The bureaucratic phenomenon*.   Chicago: Univ. of Chicago Press, 1964.

39. Crutchfield, R. S.   Conformity and character.   *Amer. Psychologist*, 1955, *10*, 191–198.

40. Dalton, M.   *Men who manage*.   New York: Wiley, 1959.

41. Day, R., and Hamblin, R.   Some effects of close and punitive styles of supervision.   *Amer. J. Sociol.*, 1964, *69*, no. 5, 499–510.

42. Dent, J. K.   Organizational correlates of the goals of business management.   *Personnel Psychol.*, 1959, *12*, 365–393.

43. Dunlop, J. T.   *Industrial relations systems*.   New York: Holt, 1959.

44. Emery, F. E., and Thorsrud, E.   *Industrial democracy*.   London: Tavistock Publications Ltd., 1965.

45. Emery, F. E., and Trist, E. L.   Socio-technical systems.   Paper presented at the 6th Annual International Meeting of the Institute of Management Sciences. Paris: September 1959.

46. Ferguson, L. L.   Social scientists in the plant.   *Harvard Bus. Rev.*, 1964, *42*, no. 3, 133–143.

47. Festinger, L., Schachter, S., and Back, K.   *Social pressures in informal groups: A study of a housing project*.   New York: Harper, 1950.

48. Festinger, L., and Thibaut, J.   Interpersonal communication in small groups.   *J. abnorm. soc. Psychol.*, 1951, *46*, 92–99.

49. Fiedler, F. E.   The influence of leader-laymen relations on combat crew effectiveness.   *J. abnorm. soc. Psychol.*, 1955, *51*, 227–235.

50. Fleishman, E.   Leadership climate, human relations training, and supervisory behavior.   In (Ed.) *Studies in personnel and in-*

dustrial psychology. Homewood, Ill.: Dorsey Press, 1961, pp. 315–328.

51. French, J. R. P., Jr. The social environment of mental health. *J. soc. Iss.*, 1963, *19*, no. 4, 39–56.

52. French, J. R. P., Jr., Israel, J., and As, D. An experiment in participation in a Norwegian factory. *Hum. Rel.*, 1960, *13*, 3–19.

53. French, J. R. P., Jr., Kay, E., and Meyer, H. H. Participation and the appraisal system. *Human Relations* (in press).

54. Friedmann, G. *Industrial society*. Glencoe, Ill.: Free Press, 1955.

55. Gilbreth, F. B. *Motion study*. New York: Van Nostrand, 1911.

56. Golembiewski, R. T. *Behavior and the organization: O and M and the Small Group*. Chicago: Rand McNally, 1962.

57. Goodwin, H. G. Work simplification. *Factory Management and Maintenance*, 1958, 72–106.

58. Gouldner, A. W. *Patterns of industrial bureaucracy*. Glencoe, Ill.: Free Press, 1954.

59. Guest, R. H. Men and machines: An assembly-line worker looks at his job. *Personnel*, 1955, *31*, 496–503.

60. Guetzkow, H. (Ed.). *Groups, leadership, and men*. Pittsburgh: Carnegie Institute of Technology, 1951.

61. Gurin, G., Veroff, J., and Feld, Sheila. *Americans view their mental health*. New York: Basic Books, 1960.

62. Haberstroh, C. Goals, programs and the training function. In (27).

63. Haire, M., Ghiselli, E., and Porter, L. W. An international study of management attitudes and democratic leadership. In *Proceedings CIOS XIII, International Management Congress*. New York: Council for International Progress in Management (USA), 1963, pp. 101–114.

64. Halpin, A., and Winer, B. A factorial study of the leader behavior descriptions. In (147) pp. 39–51.

65. Hariton, T. *Conditions influencing the effects of training foremen in new human relations principles*. Doctoral thesis, University of Michigan, 1951.

66. Harris, E., and Fleishman, E. Human relations training and the stability of leadership patterns. In Fleishman, E. (Ed.). *Studies in personnel and industrial psychology*. Homewood, Ill.: Dorsey Press, 1961, pp. 230–238.

67. Harrison, R. Impact of the laboratory on perception of others by the experimental group. In (9).

68. Hemphill, J., and Coons, A.   Development of the leader behavior description questionnaire.   In (147) pp. 6–38.

69. Herzberg, F., Mausner, B., and Snyderman, Barbara.   *The motivation to work*.   New York: Wiley, 1959.

70. Herzberg, F., Mausner, B., Peterson, R. O., and Capwell, Dora F.   *Job attitudes: Review of research and opinion*.   Pittsburgh, Pa.: Psychological Service of Pittsburgh, 1957.

71. Homans, G. C.   *The human group*.   New York: Harcourt, Brace, 1950.

72. Hugh-Jones, E. M. (Ed.).   *Human relations and modern management*.   Amsterdam: North–Holland Publ. Co., 1958.

73. Huxley, A.   *Brave new world*.   New York: Bantam, 1953.

74. James, W.   *Principles of psychology*.   New York: Holt, 1890.

75. Kahn, R. L.   Human relations on the shop floor.   In (72), Chapter 3.

76. Kahn, R. L., and Mann, F. C.   Uses of survey research in policy determination.   *Proc., Ninth Annual Meeting IRRA, 1957,* 256–274.

77. Kasl, S. V., and French, J. R. P., Jr.   The effects of occupational status on physical and mental health.   *J. soc. Issues,* 1962, *17,* no. 3, 67–89.

78. Katona, G.   Rational behavior and economic behavior.   *Psychol. Rev.,* 1953, *60,* no. 5, 307–318.

79. Katz, D., and Kahn, R. L.   Leadership practices in relation to productivity and morale.   In D. Cartwright and A. Zander (Eds.) *Group Dynamics*.   Evanston, Ill.: Row, Peterson, 1953, pp. 554–570.

80. Katz, D., and Kahn, R. L.   Some recent findings in human relations research in industry.   In G. Swanson, T. Newcomb, and E. Hartley (Eds.), *Readings in social psychology*. (2nd ed.)   New York: Holt, 1952, pp. 650–665.

81. Katz, D., Maccoby, E., and Morse, Nancy.   *Productivity, supervision and morale in an office situation*.   Ann Arbor: Institute for Social Research, Univ. of Michigan, 1950.

82. Katz, D., Maccoby, N., Gurin, G., and Floor, Lucretia.   *Productivity supervision and morale among railroad workers*.   Ann Arbor: Survey Research Center, Univ. of Michigan, 1951.

83. Katzell, R. A.   Industrial psychology.   In *Ann. Rev. of Psychol.* Palo Alto, Calif.: Annual Review Inc., 1957, pp. 243–244.

84. Kolaja, J.   *Worker's Councils, the Yugoslav experience*.   London: Tavistock Publications Ltd., 1965.

85. Krulee, G. K.   The Scanlon plan: Cooperation through participation. *The Journal of Business of the University of Chicago*, 1955, 27, no. 2, 100–113.

86. Landsberger, H. A.   *Hawthorne revisited.*   Ithaca, N.Y.: Cornell Univ., 1958.

87. Leavitt, H., and Bass, B.   Organization psychology. *Ann. Rev. Psychol.*, Palo Alto, Calif.: Annual Reviews Inc., 1964, pp. 371–398.

88. Lewin, K.   Frontiers in group dynamics: Concept, method and reality in social science.   *Hum. Rel.*, 1947, 1, 5–42.

89. Lewin, K.   Group decision and social change.   In (95) pp. 197–211.

90. Lieberman, S.   The effects of changes in roles on the attitudes of role occupants.   *Hum. Rel.*, 1956, 9, no. 4, 385–402.

91. Likert, R.   Influence and national sovereignty.   In J. G. Peatman and E. L. Hartley (Eds.), *Festschrift for Gardner Murphy*. New York: Harper, 1963.

92. Likert, R.   *New patterns of management.*   New York: McGraw-Hill, 1961.

93. Likert, R., and Seashore, S. E.   Making cost control work.   *Harvard Bus. Rev.*, 1963, 41, no. 6, 96–108.

94. Lysgaard, S.   Some problems in connection with informal organization of workers.   *Human Relations in Industry*. (Papers presented at Rome Conference) Paris: European Productivity Agency of the Organisation for European Economic Cooperation, 1956, pp. 44–48.

95. Maccoby, E. E., Newcomb, T. E., and Hartley, E. L. (Eds.)   *Readings in social psychology.*   New York: Holt, 1958.

96. McGehee, W.   And Esau was an hairy man.   *Amer. Psychologist*, 1964, 19, 799–804.

97. Maier, N. R. F.   *The appraisal interview: Objectives, methods and skills.*   New York: Wiley, 1958.

98. Maier, N. R. F.   *Principles of human relations.*   New York: Wiley, 1955.

99. Maier, N. R. F., Hoffman, L. R., Hooven, J. J., and Read, W. H.   *Superior-subordinate communication in management.*   New York: American Management Association, 1961.

100. Maier, N. R. F., Solem, A. R., and Maier, Ayesha A.   *Supervisory and executive development: A manual for role playing.*   New York: Wiley, 1964.

101. Mann, F. G.   Studying and creating change: A means to understanding social organization.   In *Research in industrial Human Re-*

lations. Madison, Wis.: Industrial Relations Research Association, 1957, 146–167.

102. Mann, F. G.   *A study of work satisfactions as a function of the discrepancy between inferred aspirations and achievement.* Ann Arbor: unpublished doctoral dissertation, Univ. of Michigan, 1953.

103. Mann, F. G., and Baumgartel, H. G.   *Absences and employee attitudes in an electric power company.* Ann Arbor: Survey Research Center, Univ. of Michigan, 1952.

104. March, J. G., and Simon, H. A.   *Organizations.* New York: Wiley, 1958.

105. Marrow, A. J.   *Behind the executive mask.* New York: American Management Association, 1964.

106. Marx, K. *Selected writings in sociology and social philosophy.* T. B. Bottomore and M. Rubel (Eds.). New York: McGraw-Hill Book Co., 1964.

107. Maslow, A. H.   A theory of human motivation. *Psychol. Rev.,* 1943, *50,* 370–396.

108. Merton, R. K.   Bureaucratic structure and personality.   In Merton, Gray, Hockey, and Selvin, *Reader in bureaucracy.* Glencoe, Ill.: Free Press, 1952.

109. Metcalf, H. and Urwick, L., (Eds.)   *Dynamic administration, the collected works of Mary Parker Follett.* New York: Harper, 1940.

110. Meyers, F.   Workers' control of industry in Europe. *Southwestern soc. sci. Quart.,* 1958, 100–111.

111. Miller, D. R.   The study of social relations: situation, identity, and social interaction. In S. Koch (Ed). *Psychology: A study of a science,* Vol. 5.   New York: McGraw-Hill, 1962, pp. 639–737.

112. Morse, Nancy.   *Satisfactions in the white-collar job.* Ann Arbor: Survey Research Center, Univ. of Michigan, 1953.

113. Morse, Nancy, and Reimer, E.   The experimental change of a major organizational variable. *J. abnorm. soc. Psychol.,* 1956, *52,* 120–129.

114. Mulder, M., and Stemerding, A.   Threat, attraction to group, and need for strong leadership; a laboratory experiment in a natural setting. *Hum. Rel.,* 1963, *16,* 317–343.

115. Nussbaum, F. L.   *A history of the economic institutions of modern Europe.* New York: Crofts and Co., 1933.

116. Odiorne, G. S.   The trouble with sensitivity training. *Training Directors J.,* October 1963.

117. Patchen, M.   Supervisory methods and group performance norms. *Admin. Sci. Quart.,* 1962, *7,* no. 3, 275–294.

118. Patchen, M., Seashore, S., and Eckerman, W. Some dealership characteristics related to change in new car sales volume. Ann Arbor: Institute for Social Research, Univ. of Michigan, 1961. Unpublished report.

119. Pelz, D. Influence: A key to effective leadership in the first-line supervisor. *Personnel,* 1952, *29,* 209–217.

120. Pfiffner, J. M., and Sherwood, F. P. *Administrative organization.* Englewood Cliffs, N.J.: Prentice-Hall, 1960.

121. Porter, L. W. Job attitudes in management: I. Perceived deficiencies in need fulfillment as a function of job level. *J. appl. Psychol.,* 1962, *46,* no. 6, 375–384.

122. Revans, R. W. Human relations, management and size. In (72) pp. 177–220.

123. Rice, A. K. *Productivity and social organization.* London: Tavistock Publications Ltd., 1958.

124. Roethlisberger, F. J., and Dickson, W. J. *Management and the worker.* Cambridge, Mass.: Harvard Univ. Press, 1964.

125. Rose, A. M. The social psychology of desertion from combat. *Amer. soc. Rev.,* 1951, *16,* 614–629.

126. Rosen, H. Desirable attributes of work: Four levels of management describe their job environments. *J. appl. Psychol.,* 1961, *45,* 155–160.

127. Ross, I. C., and Zander, A. F. Need satisfactions and employee turnover. *Personnel Psychol.,* 1957, *10,* 327–338.

128. Sarnoff, I., and Zimbardo, P. Anxiety, fear, and social affiliation. *J. abnorm. soc. Psychol.,* 1961, *62,* no. 2, 356–363.

129. Sayles, L. *Behavior of industrial work groups: Prediction and control.* New York: Wiley, 1958.

130. Schachter, S. Deviation, rejection and communication. *J. abnorm. soc. Psychol.,* 1951, *46,* 190–207.

131. Schachter, S. *The psychology of affiliation, experimental studies of the sources of gregariousness.* Stanford, Calif.: Stanford Univ. Press, 1959.

132. Seashore, S. E. *Group cohesiveness in the industrial work group.* Ann Arbor: Survey Research Center, Univ. of Michigan, 1954.

133. Seashore, S. E. The training of leaders for effective human relations. In R. Likert, and S. P. Hayes (Eds.), *Some applications of behavioral research.* Paris, Unesco, 1957, pp. 81–123.

134. Seashore, S. E., and Bowers, D. G. *Changing the structure and functioning of an organization.* Ann Arbor: Survey Research Center, Institute for Social Research, Monograph no. 33, 1963.

135. Seeman, M.   On the meaning of alienation.   *Amer. soc. Rev.,* 1959, *24,* no. 6, 783–791.

136. Sells, S.   Personnel management.   In *Ann. Rev. Psychol.,* 1964, pp. 399–420.

137. Selvin, H.   *The effects of leadership.*   Glencoe, Ill.: Free Press, 1960.

138. Selznick, P.   *TVA and the grass roots.*   Berkeley: Univ. California Press, 1953.

139. Shepard, H., and Blake, R. R.   Changing behavior through cognitive change.   *Hum. Organization,* 1961, *21,* 88–96.

140. Sherif, M.   *The psychology of social norms.*   New York: Harper, 1936.

141. Shipley, T. E., Jr., and Veroff, J.   A projective measure of need for affiliation.   In (13).

142. Simon, H.   Authority.   In (8), pp. 103–114.

143. Smith, C. G., and Tannenbaum, A. S.   Organizational control-structure: A comparative analysis.   *Hum. Rel.,* 1963, *16,* no. 4, 299–316.

144. Smith, Patricia.   The prediction of individual differences in susceptibility to industrial monotony.   *J. appl. Psychol.,* 1955, *39,* no. 5, 322–329.

145. Starbuck, W. H.   Organizational growth and development.   In J. March (Ed.), *Handbook of organizations.*   Chicago: Rand McNally, 1961, chapter 11.

146. Stock, Dorothy.   A survey of research on T-groups.   In (29) pp. 395–441.

147. Stogdill, R., and Coons, A. (Eds.).   *Leader behavior: Its description and measurement.*   Columbus, Ohio: Bureau of Business Research, Ohio State Univ. 1957.

148. Stotland, E.   Peer groups and reactions to power figures.   In D. Cartwright (Ed.), *Studies in social power.*   Ann Arbor: Institute for Social Research, Univ. of Michigan, 1959, pp. 53–68.

149. Stouffer, S., Lumsdaine, A., Williams, R., Jr., Smith, M. B., Janis, I., Star, Shirley, and Cottrell, L., Jr.   *Studies in social psychology in World War II* Vol. I. *The American soldier: Combat and its aftermath.*   Princeton, N.J.: Princeton Univ. Press, 1949.

150. Stouffer, S., Suchman, E. A., DeVinney, L. C., Star, Shirley A., and Williams, R. M., Jr.   *Studies in social psychology in World War II.* Vol. II, *The American soldier: Adjustment during army life.*   Princeton, N.J.: Princeton Univ. Press, 1949.

151. Strauss, G.   Some notes on power-equalization.   In H. Leavitt (Ed.), *The social science of organizations: Four perspectives.*   Englewood Cliffs, N.J.; Prentice-Hall, 1963, pp. 41–84.

152. Stuhr, A. W. Some outcomes of the New York employee survey. *Social science research report IV. Surveys and inventories.* Standard Oil Co. of New Jersey, 1962.

153. Sturmthal, A. *Workers councils.* Cambridge, Mass.: Harvard Univ. Press, 1964.

154. Tannenbaum, A. S. Control in organizations: Individual adjustment and organizational performance. *Adm. Sci. Quart.,* 1962, *7,* no. 2, 236–257.

155. Tannenbaum, A. S. Control and effectiveness in a voluntary organization. *Amer. J. Sociol.,* 1961, *LXVII,* no. 1, 33–46.

156. Tannenbaum, A. S. Unions. In J. March (Ed.), *Handbook of organizations.* Chicago: Rand McNally, 1965. Chapter 17.

157. Tannenbaum, A. S., and Allport, F. H. Personality structure and group structure: An interpretative study of their relationship through an event-structure hypothesis. *J. abnorm. soc. Psychol.,* 1956, *53,* no. 3, 272–280.

158. Tannenbaum, A. S., and Kahn, R. L. Organizational control structure: A general descriptive technique as applied to four local unions. *Hum. Rel.,* 1957, *10,* no. 2, 127–140.

159. Tannenbaum, A. S., and Kahn, R. L. *Participation in union locals.* Evanston, Ill.: Row Peterson, 1958.

160. Tannenbaum, A. S., and Seashore, S. Some changing conceptions and approaches to the study of persons in organizations. Paper presented at XV International Congress of Applied Psychology, Ljubljana, Yugoslavia, 1964.

161. Tannenbaum, R., Weschler, I. R., and Massarik, F. *Leadership and organization: A behavioral science approach.* New York: McGraw-Hill, 1961.

162. Taylor, F. W. *Scientific management.* New York: Harper, 1911.

163. Trist, E., and Bamforth, K. Some social and psychological consequences of the Longwall method of coal-getting. *Hum. Rel.,* 1951, *4,* no. 1, 3–38.

164. Trist, E., Higgin, G. W., Murray, H., and Pollock, A. B. *Organizational choice.* London: Tavistock Publications Ltd., 1963.

165. Turner, C. E. The test room studies in employee effectiveness. *Amer. J. pub. Health,* 1933, no. 23, 577–584.

166. Urwick, L. *The elements of administration.* New York: Harper, 1943.

167. Veroff, J. Development and validation of a projective measure of power motivation. *J. abnorm. soc. Psychol.,* 1957, *54,* 1–8.

168. Vroom, V. *Some personality determinants of the effects of participation.* Englewood Cliffs, N.J.: Prentice-Hall, 1960.

169. Vroom, V. *Work and motivation.* New York: Wiley, 1964.

170. Walker, C. R. *Modern technology and civilization.* New York: McGraw-Hill, 1962.

171. Walker, C. R., and Guest, R. H. The man on the assembly line. *Harvard Bus. Rev.,* 1952, *30,* 71–83.

172. Weber, M. The essentials of bureaucratic organization: An ideal-type construction. In Merton, Gray, Hockey and Selvin (Eds.), *Reader in bureaucracy.* Glencoe, Ill.: Free Press, 1952.

173. Weber, M. *The theory of social and economic organization.* New York: Oxford Univ. Press, 1947 (trans. by A. M. Henderson and Talcott Parsons, Ed. Talcott Parsons).

174. Welker, W. I. Some determinants of play and exploration in chimpanzees. *J. comp. physiol. Psychol.,* 1956, *49,* 84–89.

175. White, R., and Lippitt, R. *Autocracy and democracy: An experimental inquiry.* New York: Harper, 1960.

176. Whyte, W. F., Dalton, M., Roy, D., Sayles, L., Collins, O., Miller, F., Strauss, G., Fuerstenberg, F., and Bavelas, A. *Money and motivation: An analysis of incentives in industry.* New York: Harper, 1955.

177. Whyte, W. H., Jr. *Organization man.* New York: Simon and Schuster, 1956.

178. Wilensky, H. Human relations in the workplace: An appraisal of some recent research. In (8) pp. 25–50.

179. Worthy, J. C. Commentary on Mr. Wilensky's chapter. In (8) pp. 51–54.

180. Worthy, J. C. Factors influencing employee morale. *Harvard Bus. Rev.,* 1950, *28,* no. 1, 61–73.

index